W9-BZC-408

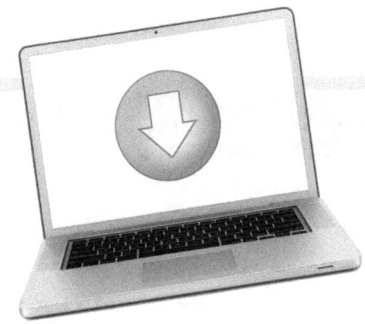

This Book Comes With Lots of
FREE Online Resources

Nolo's award-winning website has a page dedicated just to this book. Here you can:

KEEP UP TO DATE. When there are important changes to the information in this book, we'll post updates.

GET DISCOUNTS ON NOLO PRODUCTS. Get discounts on hundreds of books, forms, and software.

READ BLOGS. Get the latest info from Nolo authors' blogs.

LISTEN TO PODCASTS. Listen to authors discuss timely issues on topics that interest you.

WATCH VIDEOS. Get a quick introduction to a legal topic with our short videos.

And that's not all.
Nolo.com contains thousands of articles on everyday legal and business issues, plus a plain-English law dictionary, all written by Nolo experts and available for free. You'll also find more useful **books, software, online apps, downloadable forms,** plus a **lawyer directory.**

With
**Downloadable
FORMS**

 NOLO
LAW for ALL
Get forms and more at
www.nolo.com/back-of-book/TECH.html

☩ NOLO **The Trusted Name**
(but don't take our word for it)

"In Nolo you can trust."
THE NEW YORK TIMES

"Nolo is always there in a jam as the nation's premier publisher of do-it-yourself legal books."
NEWSWEEK

"Nolo publications…guide people simply through the how, when, where and why of the law."
THE WASHINGTON POST

"[Nolo's]…material is developed by experienced attorneys who have a knack for making complicated material accessible."
LIBRARY JOURNAL

"When it comes to self-help legal stuff, nobody does a better job than Nolo…"
USA TODAY

"The most prominent U.S. publisher of self-help legal aids."
TIME MAGAZINE

"Nolo is a pioneer in both consumer and business self-help books and software."
LOS ANGELES TIMES

5th Edition

Smart Policies for Workplace Technologies

Email, Social Media, Cell Phones & More

Lisa Guerin, J.D.

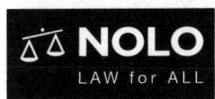

FIFTH EDITION	JANUARY 2017
Editor	MARCIA STEWART
Cover Design	SUSAN PUTNEY
Proofreading	IRENE BARNARD
Index	JULIE SHAWVAN
Printing	BANG PRINTING

Names: Guerin, Lisa, 1964- author.

Title: Smart policies for workplace technologies : email, social media, cell phones & more / Lisa Guerin, J.D.

Description: 5th Edition. | Berkeley, CA : Nolo, 2017. | Revised edition of the author's Smart policies for workplace technologies, 2015. | Includes index.

Identifiers: LCCN 2016031702 (print) | LCCN 2016045009 (ebook) | ISBN 9781413323535 (pbk.) | ISBN 9781413323542 (ebook)

Subjects: LCSH: Personal Internet use in the workplace. | Business enterprises--Computer networks--Security measures. | Telecommunication. | Blogs. | Personnel management. | Labor laws and legislation--United States.

Classification: LCC HF5549.5.P39 G84 2017 (print) | LCC HF5549.5.P39 (ebook) | DDC 651.7--dc23

LC record available at https://lccn.loc.gov/2016031702

This book covers only United States law, unless it specifically states otherwise.

Please note

We believe accurate, plain-English legal information should help you solve many of your own legal problems. But this text is not a substitute for personalized advice from a knowledgeable lawyer. If you want the help of a trained professional—and we'll always point out situations in which we think that's a good idea—consult an attorney licensed to practice in your state.

About the Author

Lisa Guerin is the author or coauthor of several Nolo books, including *The Manager's Legal Handbook, Dealing With Problem Employees: A Legal Guide, The Essential Guide to Federal Employment Laws, The Essential Guide to Workplace Investigations: How to Handle Employee Complaints & Problems, Create Your Own Employee Handbook: A Legal & Practical Guide for Employers, The Essential Guide to Family & Medical Leave,* and *The Employee Performance Handbook: Smart Strategies for Coaching Employees.* Ms. Guerin has practiced employment law in government, public interest, and private practice, where she represented clients at all levels of state and federal courts and in agency proceedings. She is a graduate of Boalt Hall School of Law at the University of California at Berkeley.

Table of Contents

Appendix

Introduction:
Why You Need Technology Policies

I n the not-so-distant past, every telephone had a cord tethering the caller to a nearby wall. The only way a business could transmit a document was to place it in an envelope and pay someone to carry it to the recipient. To research important data, we had to find the right books, sometimes by traveling to a library, then take them off the shelf, open them, and hope that the table of contents would point us to the relevant pages.

For anyone under the age of 30, these must seem like some outdated and inefficient limitations for operating a business. These days, smartphones, email, the Internet, cloud computing, and other innovations have brought huge gains in business efficiency and productivity, allowing instant communication and access to information that would have seemed unimaginable only a short time ago.

And of course, the technology wave hasn't crested yet. Every time we turn around, there's a new device—or an innovative way to use something we've already got—that could revolutionize the way we work. One day, not too long from now, we'll look back on iPhones, Twitter, and spam with the same nostalgia we reserve for the inkwell, carbon paper, and the IBM Selectric.

The Risks Posed by Technology

No matter how technology evolves, one thing remains constant: New technology brings new risks for employers. Technology can always be misused, either intentionally or accidentally. And, because employers are often legally responsible for the acts of their employees, technological developments have exponentially increased the possibility of legal exposure.

In recent years, we've been inundated with tales of employer woes: private customer information accidentally made public; racist or sexist jokes transmitted through a company's email system; employees causing car accidents while doing business on their phones; employees or officers "outed" as the authors of glowing online reviews of company products; and employees airing workplace gripes on social networking sites. Although technology has promised to increase efficiency and rid us of documentation, it sometimes seems to have had the opposite effect. For example, companies now spend thousands of dollars combing through their electronic files to produce evidence for auditors, courts, and government agencies.

How does an employer modulate this digital din? Some try to control technology with other technology, such as software that blocks certain Internet sites, programs that scan email for illegal content, or ever-changing digital passwords to prevent theft of company data and secrets. But fighting technology with technology is a never-ending game of cat and mouse, as the makers of anti-spam software have learned. There's always a way to skirt these technological solutions, which means companies have to develop a response to the workaround, and the escalation continues.

How Technology Policies Can Help

Rather than fighting tech with more tech, a better approach is to adopt a set of commonsense rules that explain how employees should use the technologies the company makes available to them. Of course, policies alone won't stop all employee misconduct: There will always be employees who act badly, no matter what your company's handbook says. But policies, combined with training, leadership by example, and consistent enforcement, will help your company make sure that employees are using its electronic resources as the company intends.

And, if an employee doesn't follow the rules, policies provide a strong measure of legal protection if your company has to discipline or fire the employee, or prove that it did everything it could to prevent the incident (in the unfortunate event someone was harmed by an employee's misuse of technology).

Using This Book

This book provides policies you can adapt for your workplace on email use, employee blogs, posting to company-sponsored social media pages, using cellphones for work, downloading software,

Internet access, and much more. It also provides the information you need to decide whether to use a particular policy and how to customize it to fit your workplace.

After Chapter 1 explains what technology policies can do for your company and how to draft them effectively, each subsequent chapter addresses a specific device or function, from software to smartphones to social media. These chapters explain common problems employers face, examine the rapidly changing legal landscape for employee use of technology, and provide sample language you can use to draft or revise your company's technology policies.

This book is intended for owners, managers, and human resources specialists at companies of all sizes, from those with only a few employees on up. As you'll see, even the smallest employers should start considering technology policies once they have a handful of employees who use computers, smartphones, or other tech devices to do their jobs. You can use this book to come up with your company's first set of tech policies or to troubleshoot an employee handbook that's been in use for years. Either way, as explained in Chapter 1, you'll need to run your finished product by a lawyer. State laws on tech and privacy vary, and the laws addressing these twenty-first century issues are in a nearly constant state of evolution. A lawyer can help you make sure your policies are fully up to date and comply with all applicable laws.

Get Policy Language, Updates, and More on Nolo.com

This book is filled with sample policy language you can use to create your own technology policies. You can access it in digital form—along with an acknowledgment form—at this book's online companion page:

www.nolo.com/back-of-book/TECH.html

You'll find other useful information on that page too, such as updates and blog posts.

Drafting Effective Technology Policies

Your company probably has some written policies gathered in an employee handbook or policy manual, covering things like time off, benefits, employee conduct, and termination procedures. Unfortunately, however, many companies have neglected to keep up with the times by creating policies dealing with technology. Sometimes, the company's decision makers don't understand how technological innovations work or don't know how employees are actually using company resources. Sometimes, policy makers assume that existing policies are adequate to cover new technologies. Perhaps most often, however, the people responsible for writing policies just have too many other things to do, and put off updating their handbook to a later date.

> **CAUTION**
> **Practice makes policy.** A policy can exist without being written down or even communicated orally to employees. For example, if everyone in a company, from senior management on down, uses the company's email system for personal messages, that's company policy, even if the company has no official written guidelines saying that it's okay to use email in this way. The company would have a tough time defending a decision to fire an employee for sending personal messages if everyone else did so with impunity. It's much better to consciously decide what your company's policies should be than to create policies by default.

How Technology Policies Can Help Your Company

If your company has procrastinated on drafting or updating its technology policies, you're missing an opportunity to protect the company's assets and leaving yourselves open to legal trouble in the future. Here are some ways that well-drafted technology policies can help your company.

Protect Trade Secrets

Employees stealing trade secrets once had to stand over a copy machine, smuggle out boxes of documents, or bring in cameras. Today, however, the valuable intangible information upon which many companies are built—their trade secrets—can easily be purloined in digital format.

Technology policies can help protect against loss of company trade secrets, whether it occurs intentionally—as when an employee steals data to sell to a competitor or start a similar business—or unintentionally—as when an employee sends confidential information through Web-based email, which is hacked by an outsider, or stores sensitive files on a smartphone that is later stolen.

Even if your company faces an aggressive trade secret thief who doesn't care about the rules, strong policy language will help your company show that it took steps to protect its confidential information, which will work in your company's favor when it tries to stop others from using its stolen secrets. When deciding whether particular information qualifies for trade secret protection, courts look at how hard the company worked to try to keep that information confidential. The more safeguards you have in place, the more likely you are to prevail in court, even if your secrets were stolen despite your best efforts.

Promote Your Company Effectively

These days, consumers look for information about products and services online. Your company's official Internet presence—on its own website, in company blogs, and on the company's social media pages—plays a significant role in creating and maintaining your company's reputation. And, its "unofficial" presence—in personal blogs and posts, online reviews, or YouTube videos, for example—may be just as important, for better or for worse. Policies that draw clear lines on what employees should and shouldn't say online, whether in company-authorized content or in personal posts, can help you make sure that your company is being represented positively and appropriately in cyberspace.

Preserve Customer and Employee Privacy

All companies keep some confidential information about their employees, whether Social Security numbers, next of kin, or medical records. Many companies also have confidential customer information, such as addresses, telephone numbers, and credit card accounts. Companies have a legal obligation (and obvious incentive) to maintain the privacy of this information, which up-to-date technology policies will help you do. Many states also require companies to notify consumers if their information is leaked, stolen, or otherwise compromised.

Nearly 900 Million Breached Records ... and Counting

A stolen laptop here, a hacked website there, and the security breaches start to add up. According to the Privacy Rights Clearinghouse, more than 900 million records were compromised between January 2005 and July 2016, and the number is increasing by the thousands daily. The Clearinghouse keeps an extensive database of security breaches involving consumer information (you can view it at www.privacyrights.org; select "Data Breaches" from the home page).

Lay the Groundwork for Discipline and Termination

Policies provide the basis for employee discipline and termination by explaining what conduct is prohibited. Although most companies have the right to fire employees at will (that is, for any reason that's not illegal), it's always wise, for legal and practical reasons, to fire only for good cause. By putting employees on notice, technology policies make it more difficult for employees to later argue that they were treated unfairly or that they didn't know their conduct was prohibited.

Lessons From the Real World

Violating company policy isn't necessarily a crime.

David Nosal quit his job at Korn/Ferry, an executive search firm. He got some of his former coworkers to access Korn/Ferry's database, using their own log-in credentials, and download lists of sources, names, and contact information. He used this information to start his own competing business.

Nosal was charged by the federal government on 20 criminal counts, including conspiracy, mail fraud, theft of trade secrets, and violation of the Computer Fraud and Abuse Act (CFAA). Among other things, the CFAA makes it a crime to "exceed authorized access" by accessing "a computer with authorization and [using] such access to obtain or alter information in the computer that the accesser is not entitled so to obtain or alter."

The federal government argued that Nosal had conspired, with his former coworkers, to violate the CFAA. Korn/Ferry's computer policies prohibit employees from disclosing confidential company information. Therefore, even though the coworkers were authorized to access and use the information in the database, they exceeded that authorized access when they handed trade secrets over to a competitor.

The federal Court of Appeals for the Ninth Circuit disagreed with this argument, however. Making company policy the determining factor in whether an employee's conduct is illegal would potentially criminalize everything from sending personal email from work to checking the weather. Outside the employment context, the Court pointed out that violating the terms of service of any online business, from Facebook to Amazon to eHarmony, could potentially result in criminal charges. Although Nosal could still be subject to civil liability for stealing trade secrets, violating his contract, and more, he could not be prosecuted under the CFAA.

United States v. Nosal, 676 F.3d 854 (9th Cir. 2011).

CAUTION

Policies must be enforced consistently. Having policies on paper is a good first step, but it isn't enough to protect your company from wrongful termination lawsuits. To use a policy as a lawsuit defense strategy, your company must be able to show that everyone who violated the policy faced the same consequences. Otherwise, an employee can use your company's selective enforcement as proof of discrimination, retaliation, or other unfair treatment.

Tell Employees That Their Communications Aren't Private

Because your company may one day have to read or monitor employee email messages and Internet browsing histories, you should put employees on notice. It's only fair to tell employees ahead of time that their messages may be read. Notifying employees about monitoring will also deter them from sending inappropriate messages in the first place. What's more, employees' legal right to privacy is determined, in part, by how much privacy they reasonably expect to have. If your company tells employees their communications aren't private, it will be hard for them to argue later that they nonetheless expected confidentiality.

Avoid Problems Caused by Employee Mistakes

Many of the problems created by workplace technology are the result of inadvertent errors—for example, clicking on an attachment that unleashes a virus or posting confidential information when answering a customer question online—not intentional missteps. By setting ground rules for employees and explaining why those rules are important, technology policies can help your company avoid many of these problems in the first place.

Lessons From the Real World

Company can read email, even if the employee has a confidential password.

In one of the first cases to address workplace email, a California court adopted the rule that virtually all courts since have followed: Employee use of company email is not private. The case was brought by Bonita Bourke, whom Nissan hired to help employees with problems related to the company's computer system.

The first sign of trouble was during a training session. In trying to demonstrate how dealership management could use email effectively, one of Ms. Bourke's coworkers pulled up a message at random to use as a teaching tool. Unfortunately for Ms. Bourke, it was a personal, sexual message that she had sent to another employee.

After the incident was reported to management, the company reviewed the entire workgroup's email messages. It found a number of personal messages, including messages with sexual overtones, sent by Ms. Bourke, who was fired.

Ms. Bourke sued Nissan for violating her privacy rights, among other things. The court ruled against her, however. Ms. Bourke had signed a form indicating her understanding that company policy restricted use of company computers to business purposes only. She also knew that email messages were occasionally read by someone other than the intended recipient. The court therefore found that, even though Ms. Bourke had a confidential password to use her computer, she could not reasonably expect her email messages to be private.

Bourke v. Nissan Motor Corp., No B068705 (California Court of Appeal, 2nd District, 1993).

Conserve Company Resources

Misuse of technology—whether in the form of streaming video, visiting illicit websites, or sending excessive personal email—costs time and money. Your company can preserve its bandwidth and server capacity, and maintain higher employee productivity, by adopting policies that limit how employees may use its technological resources.

Employers' Duty to Retain and Hand Over Electronic Evidence

In 2006, federal rules took effect that define the obligations of lawsuit opponents to save and provide electronically stored evidence. The Federal Rules of Civil Procedure (FRCP), which apply to all noncriminal federal lawsuits, were updated to reflect that modern business documents are more likely to be stored on a server, flash drive, or backup tape—or in the cloud—than in a filing cabinet.

The FRCP now explicitly includes electronically stored information in the categories of documents and evidence that must be exchanged in discovery: the process of requesting and receiving information from the other side and from witnesses in a lawsuit. The rules have always obligated parties to discuss the case and exchange key evidence and witness lists early on. Now, electronically stored information must be discussed and produced at this meeting, which is supposed to take place only a few months after a lawsuit is filed.

The rules impose a heavy obligation on companies to properly organize their electronic information so it can be accessed and reviewed quickly for a lawsuit. However, there's some good news here for companies that routinely purge emails and electronic information: There's no penalty if a party can't provide electronic data because it was lost as a result of the routine, good faith operation of an information system. But this "safe harbor" provision applies only until litigation is in the offing. Companies facing a lawsuit must immediately stop their purging, shredding, and deleting, and impose a "litigation hold." A company that destroys potentially relevant evidence after a lawsuit is imminent can face huge fines and penalties.

Limit Liability for Employee Misconduct

In some situations, your company can use its policies to show that it tried to prevent harm to others. For example, if your company has a written policy prohibiting employees from making business-related calls while driving, that policy can be used as evidence that the company shouldn't be legally responsible for injuries an employee caused while doing just that.

Manage Electronic Documents

Most of the innovations covered in this book allow employees to create, modify, and transmit documents electronically. They also create their own electronic records, in the form of logs, user records, browsing history, address books, and so on. Employers have a duty to preserve and hand over electronic documents like these in a lawsuit, just as if they were pieces of paper. Without policies telling employees how to manage their electronic documents, your company won't be able to meet these obligations. Lawsuits aside, if employees don't know which electronic documents to keep and where to put them, your company might not be able to access important records like contracts and customer orders.

Creating Your Policies

This book will help you draft and update technology policies that will be effective in your company. What this book can't do, however, is tell you which policies are right for your company: That will depend on your industry, your corporate culture, the sophistication of your employees, your company's comfort level with risk, and plenty of other intangibles that will vary from company to company.

A large part of your job will be to decide how intrusive or trusting your company wants to be with its employees. This issue comes up again and again in the technology field because employee use of each of these devices and functions can be monitored. Here are some questions you may have to consider:

- Will your company read every employee email message or will it simply reserve its right to monitor email if it needs to?
- Will your company block access to certain Internet sites, monitor employee Internet traffic, or just tell employees not to visit certain types of sites?
- Will your company allow—or ask—employees to use personal phones and other electronic devices for work or prohibit them from doing so?

What Does IT Do?

Information technology (IT) expertise can be enormously valuable in helping your company choose the right tech equipment to meet its needs; install, set up, implement, or roll out that equipment; train employees in using the equipment; troubleshoot problems with the equipment; and help management decide when it's time to upgrade or replace that equipment. IT can also help with information management by, for example, implementing systems to safeguard private customer information (like credit card numbers and medical records); dealing with outside vendors and partners (such as companies that provide cloud computing, software for tracking sales or employee work hours, or apps for mobile devices); and making sure employees are using technology appropriately (by, for example, monitoring employee email or Internet use). By staying on top of new products and trends in the field (and how they can enhance or even change the way your company works or the products and services it provides), IT experts can even help shape your company's strategic planning.

Many established companies already have IT departments, particularly in industries that have to keep customer information secure or deal with technology as a product or service. Even if your company doesn't have dedicated IT staff on payroll, it likely has had some IT help, perhaps from a consultant or just a tech-savvy employee. After all, a company will need to set up a network, decide on how and where to store digital information, and perhaps set up and manage a website. It will also need someone to call in a hurry if any of those functions stops working.

What Does IT Do? (continued)

If your company is looking for IT help, the options include:

- **Hiring a consultant.** Many small companies hire a freelancer to recommend, set up, and maintain their technical systems, and be available to train employees, update those systems, and troubleshoot as needed. This might make sense for very small companies that don't have sophisticated tech needs.
- **Contracting with a managed service provider (MSP).** An MSP is an outside company that contracts with a client business to remotely provide the IT services the client needs. An MSP can handle cloud computing, applications and software management, storage, data recovery after a disaster, and more. Using an MSP can give your company access to tech expertise and services as you need them, without having to dedicate your staff to these issues.
- **Hire IT employees.** As your company grows, and particularly if it has significant IT needs, your company may decide to hire its own IT staff. This could make sense if, for example, your company must maintain sensitive customer or client information, your company provides tech services or products, or you want to work closely with technology experts in designing individualized systems for your company.

No matter which of these IT options your company chooses, you will want to involve anyone who helps with your company's tech in the policy planning process.

Each chapter in this book covers a different type of electronic resource or function, such as email, smartphones, or social media, providing an overview of the most important issues to consider, sample policy language, and information that will help your company decide whether—and how much—to regulate employee use of that equipment.

Although some policies should be adopted in every company (prohibiting employees from texting while driving, for example), others are not so universal. That's why your first step in crafting technology policies is not to open this book to the appropriate chapter, but instead to figure out what your company is already doing and what it wants to do.

Determine Your Current Practices

To get started, find out how technology is being used and regulated in your company now. First, consult your company's employee handbook or other written policies. Does your company have policies in place dealing with email, blogs, cellphones, and the other tech addressed in this book? Are these policies up to date and adequate to address everything your company and its employees currently use? Does your company require employees to sign acknowledgment forms demonstrating that they have received, read, and understood these policies?

Once you've collected and reviewed your company's written policies, it's time to get out of your office and talk to people to find out what types of technology are actually in use, and in what ways. Here are some ideas to help you get started:

- **Talk to your IT department** (if your company has one). Find out what technologies your company supports and what it prohibits. Does IT have the capacity to read employee email and instant messages or to track employee Internet use? Is someone actually reading employee communications? Does the company block access to certain websites? Does the company provide cellphones, smartphones, or laptops to employees? Does it allow—or require—employees to use their own electronic devices for work? If so, are there any limits on the makes or models, or on an employee's ability to access the company's network? Is IT aware of any problems in employee use or misuse of equipment?

- **Interview company managers.** What technological resources do they use in their departments? Do they issue equipment to employees? Do they encourage employees to purchase their own equipment to use for work? Are they concerned about employee use of technology? Have they had to discipline or fire any employees for misusing electronic resources? What types of equipment do they need for their departments to function most efficiently and productively?

Electronic Monitoring at Work

The American Management Association (AMA) has been surveying employers about their monitoring of employee activity since 2001. The most recent survey, for 2007, reveals that many employers monitor employee email and Internet activity. Here's what employers were looking at:

- **Email.** 43% of the companies surveyed monitor employee email. Almost ¾ of those use technology to automatically review messages, and 40% have an actual human being read email. Perhaps as a result of this monitoring, 28% of the companies who responded to the survey had fired someone for misuse of email, mostly in the form of inappropriate or offensive language or violation of company rules.
- **Internet use.** Of the companies surveyed, ⅔ monitor employee Internet connections, and the same number block certain sites. 30% of the companies had fired someone for Internet misuse, with the vast majority of terminations resulting from viewing, downloading, or uploading inappropriate or offensive material.
- **Computer use.** 45% of the companies track content, keystrokes, and time spent at the keyboard, and almost the same number review computer files.
- **Outside sites.** 12% of responding companies monitor blogs to find out what's being said about them, and 10% monitor social networking sites.

- **Meet with the online team.** Talk to the employees who oversee your company's online presence and find out what your company is doing on the Internet. Is it active in social media channels? Does it have business blogs? If so, how does it handle reader comments? Are you podcasting or producing online video? Does the company keep track of what others are saying about it online? The answers to these questions will help you figure out whether and how you need to address employee contributions—whether official or unofficial—to the company's online presence.
- **Consult with the lawyers.** Talk to your company's attorney to find out whether there are any special concerns—or past problems—you'll need to address. Has the company had to discipline or fire employees for electronic misconduct? Are there special concerns in your industry that you should consider? Do your state's laws or applicable court decisions address privacy and technology?
- **Get feedback from employees.** Find out what employees are really doing. Although you could talk directly to employees, you'll probably get more accurate results with an anonymous survey or questionnaire. Your goal is to find out how employees are really using the available technology. In a face-to-face interview, few employees will admit to things like sending personal email, visiting websites that aren't related to work, or getting around the company's electronic controls.

Draft Policies

Don't be surprised or concerned if your interviews revealed confusion about your company's current policies and expectations, or differences in the way technology is used or managed in different departments. Your job now is to use that information to come up with policies that will work for the whole company and be enforced consistently in the future.

For each type of technology your company uses, go to the appropriate chapter in this book and review the policy language provided. Some chapters include alternatives to choose from, depending on how your company wants to handle a particular issue; some also include optional language you can include if, for example, you use monitoring software or provide employees with hands-free telephone equipment. Each chapter starts with a checklist of policy provisions, so you can make sure you've considered every important issue. Most readers should be able to put together effective policies using the language provided in the book and on the online companion page, with very few changes.

If, however, your company requires a different approach or wants to address additional concerns, you may need to draft or modify policy language. Here are a few rules to keep in mind:

- **Keep it simple.** Use short sentences and paragraphs, and easily understood vocabulary. Be as clear and concise as possible.
- **Know your audience.** Write in the language and style that reflects the culture of your company, and the education and sophistication of its employees.
- **Explain the policy.** When writing a technology policy, it's especially important to explain the purpose behind it. Employees who don't understand why it's important not to, for example, open an unscanned email attachment, send confidential information through Web-based email, or post "anonymous" reviews of your company's products, might assume the company is just being paternalistic in imposing these requirements. Employees who know why a policy is necessary are more likely to follow it (and less likely to use workarounds).

Review and Revise Policies

Once you've come up with draft policies, get some feedback. Ask the IT department and your company's managers to read them; they are the ones who are going to have to actually enforce the policies and field employee questions. They can let you know whether they think it will be difficult to implement a particular policy.

Wearable Tech, for Work and Play

For several years now, the "next big thing" in tech has been wearables: devices we attach to our bodies. Fitness tracking wristbands, smart watches, and computerized headsets (like Google Glass) have become more commonplace, at work and at home. And employers have had to adapt to the use and misuse of these devices in the workplace.

Privacy and trade secret protection have been major concerns as these technologies come to work. Because of their small size, these devices can easily record meetings at which new products are discussed or photograph other employees without their knowledge, for example. And, if employees use their personal devices to connect to your company's network, data security could be compromised.

On the other hand, a number of employers are putting wearable tech to work. For example, employees who need both hands to do their jobs can use a computerized headset to receive instructions and information (sometimes, directly from a vehicle, machine, or piece of equipment that is a card-carrying member of the Internet of Things). Employees who need instant access to information about stock, inventory, deliveries, and orders can get it easily, without breaking stride. Employees can communicate with each other or with company databases—for instance, to get information about important customers or clients—unobtrusively.

Wearable tech also allows employers to track employees like never before, keeping tabs not only on their movements through the workplace and beyond, but also employee productivity and even their vital signs. This monitoring capability disturbs employees and privacy advocates, and it's no wonder why. Who wants their every move tracked, whether on or off the job? And, once this information is gathered, there's also the problem of keeping it safe. For example, could the government subpoena an employer's records of employee movements? The legal battles over these technologies are just getting started, so stay tuned.

After you've considered this feedback and revised your policies, it's time to get a final review from a lawyer to be sure your technology policies are legally sound and up to date. Don't skip this important step. Technology—and the legal rules governing it—changes at the speed of light. State laws vary on what's allowed and what's prohibited when it comes to employee privacy. A lawyer can help you make sure your policies are current and effective. A final legal review like this shouldn't take much time (or cost much money).

CAUTION

The National Labor Relations Board (NLRB) is closely reviewing technology policies. In recent years, the government agency most likely to challenge an employer's technology policies is the NLRB, which interprets and enforces labor laws. The NLRB has overturned email policies, social media policies, confidentiality policies, and more as unfairly restricting employees' rights to discuss the terms and conditions of their employment. In 2015, the General Counsel of the NLRB released a memorandum that calls into question some common handbook provisions, including rules on use of technology. This rapidly changing terrain is just one more reason why you must have a lawyer review your tech policies before putting them into place.

RESOURCE

Need help with other employment policies? If you're looking for employment policies on everything from hiring, wages and hours, discrimination, employee conduct, and more, Nolo's got you covered. You can find forms, sample policies, and modifications that allow you to tailor policies to the needs of your business in *Create Your Own Employee Handbook: A Legal & Practical Guide for Employers*, by Lisa Guerin and Amy DelPo (Nolo).

Distribute Policies and Acknowledgment Forms

Now, it's time to pass out the policies. You should follow that with a meeting where you explain the policies and answer any questions employees might have. Tell employees that the company expects them to read the policies and abide by them, and ask employees to sign an acknowledgment form to that effect. An acknowledgment form is available on this book's online companion page; see the appendix for information on accessing it, and a sample is shown below.

> **CAUTION**
> **Acknowledgment forms may be legally required.** Acknowledgment forms may look like overkill or a simple exercise in paperwork, but they are a vitally important part of your technology strategy. Currently, at least one state requires employers to get written consent from employees before monitoring their email and Internet use, and other states consider similar legislation every year. Even if they aren't legally required where your company does business, acknowledgment forms ensure that employees understand the rules for electronic communications, which will result in fewer violations of those rules and more protection for your company if it ever has to defend a decision to read employee communications.

It's a good idea to meet with employees to discuss any changes or additions to those policies. Use of technology is an area of major interest to employees, and one in which you may meet resistance. At a meeting, you can explain why the company needs these policies and what employees will have to do to comply.

Enforce Policies

Your policies are only as good as the paper they're printed on unless your company puts them into action. Ignoring policy violations is a quick way to undo all of your work. Not only does it signal to employees that they don't have to follow the rules, but it also creates extra legal exposure. Adopting a policy shows that your company understands the risks of misusing a particular technology. If it ignores policy violations,

Sample Electronic Communications and Equipment Policy Acknowledgment

My signature on this form indicates that I have read the Company's [*list the titles of all technology policies your company has adopted, such as "Computer and Software Policy, Email Policy, Internet Policy, and Cellphone Policy"*], and I agree to abide by their terms. I understand that any communications I send or receive using Company equipment, including but not limited to email, instant messages, and text messages, are not private, and that the Company may access, monitor, read, and/or copy those messages at any time, for any reason. I also understand that the Company reserves the right to monitor my use of the Internet, and that such monitoring may occur at any time, for any reason.

I understand that all electronic equipment issued to me by the Company, including but not limited to [*list all types of equipment issued to employees, such as "computers, cellphones, laptops, smartphones, and personal digital assistants"*], belong to the Company, and that I must return such equipment upon the Company's request. I also understand that the Company reserves the right to monitor my use of this equipment, and that such monitoring may occur at any time, for any reason.

_____   _____

Employee Signature   Date

_____

Employee Name (print)

Lessons From the Real World

Adopting technology policies doesn't make your company liable for employee abuse.

It all started when David Sigler yelled at Thomas Kobinsky for letting his child relieve himself in the Siglers' yard. Kobinsky struck back by using his work computer to place public ads for a business Sigler didn't have, order products and subscriptions for the Siglers, and search the Internet for information about them. He also called their workplace on his company cellphone.

The Siglers sued Kobinsky and his employer, CUNA Mutual Insurance Society (CUNA), apparently the deeper pocket. The Siglers argued that, because CUNA had a policy forbidding personal use of computer resources, and because it had previously disciplined a number of employees for Internet offenses, it had a legal duty to monitor employees and review their Internet activities.

A Wisconsin court of appeals rejected the Siglers' claims. The court found that it wasn't reasonably foreseeable that giving employees Internet access would result in Kobinsky's bizarre revenge campaign. The court also found that allowing the lawsuit to proceed would expand liability to such an extent that all employers would be turned into insurers of their employees' online conduct. Having policies and requiring employees to certify that they had read and would comply with those policies was enough to meet the employer's general duty of care to the public.

Sigler v. Kobinsky and CUNA Mutual Insurance Society, 762 N.W. 2d 706 (2008).

your company is essentially saying, "We understand that this could create problems, but we've decided not to do anything about it."

For example, suppose company policy says employees will be issued hands-free equipment and must use it when driving and talking on a cellphone for business. The company hands out cellphones, but decides to put off purchasing headsets until the next fiscal year. An employee hits a pedestrian while taking a sales call. Here's what the pedestrian's lawyer might ask the human resources manager: "You wrote these policies, correct? And you said employees have to use hands-free technology because your company recognizes that's safer than allowing them to use handheld phones while driving, right? But your company never purchased hands-free devices, did it? And now, my client has been permanently injured because your company didn't want to spend $500, isn't that right?"

Review Policies and Update If Necessary

If you're in charge of keeping your company's employee handbook up to date, you probably don't read it from cover to cover when a review is required; you review only policies that may need to be changed because of a court ruling, new statute, or change in company practice. The truth is that most company policies aren't going to change from year to year.

In the technology arena, however, things change quickly and you may find these policies need review once or twice a year. When you adopt a new policy or change the company's existing policy, meet with employees to explain what's new. As you did when you initially rolled out your tech policies, you should give employees time to read the policy, tell them why it was adopted, and answer any questions they might have. You should also prepare a new acknowledgment form.

Keep in mind, too, that this is just the beginning. Every year, there are new technology-related concerns on the horizon and your company's policies should address these issues as soon as they hit your radar screen.

Considering New Technology?

After reading this book, you'll have a good idea of the kinds of issues you need to consider and address in your tech policies. You can use that expertise to help inform the company's decisions about new technology. Rather than just introducing a new gadget and waiting for the fallout, your company can plan ahead to avoid future problems. Here are some questions to brainstorm when your company is looking into new electronic resources:

- Why do we need this technology? Knowing how you want employees to use a particular device will help you make more informed decisions about purchasing, functionality, and appropriate limits for employees.
- Will we supply it for employees? If so, you'll have to think about how you will decide who gets one and whether you will limit personal use. If not, will you reimburse employees who purchase their own device? How will you limit security risks of employees linking to your network from, or keeping business information on, a personal device?
- Who will use this technology? If only the most senior management will be using a particular device, for example, your company may decide to forgo monitoring or extensive rules about personal use.
- What risks are associated with this technology? Are there new data security issues to consider? Safety concerns? A high risk of theft (as is true with many smaller devices) or abuse?
- What records does the device create? Because most technology creates a record, you'll need to consider whether your company should keep those records and in what form.
- Do we want to monitor employee use of the technology? If so, you'll need to make sure you have the resources and capability to handle it.

Computers and Software

In This Chapter:

Policy Provisions for Computers and Software

☐ Use of Computer Equipment

☐ Remote Access

☐ Encryption and Encoding

☐ Software Use

A lthough many of us think of computers and the Internet as being joined at the hip, the computer—sans the Internet connection—remains a crucial business tool. Most U.S. employees have computers, which they use to write documents, populate spreadsheets, design graphics and artwork, put together presentations, track financial records, and more.

Because employees do the bulk of their work—and store it—on company computers, your company's policies must address several concerns. First, your company must be able to access its digital records and data if and when it needs to. Second, your company must protect its investments and make sure that computer equipment is not misused. Finally, your company must make sure that employees don't illegally use, copy, or download software programs.

The High Cost of Software Piracy

When employees download pirated software, they may also be inadvertently downloading malware to your company's system. According to the Business Software Alliance (BSA), this happens more often than we might think: Almost 40% of all software in use worldwide—at a commercial value of more than $52 billion—is unlicensed. These international figures are significantly higher than the figures for the United States, where about 17% of our software is unlicensed, at a total value of about $9 billion.

Computers

Your computer use policy must address only a few basic issues; most of the details can be left to your other policies on specific computer activities such as email (discussed in Chapter 3), Internet access (discussed in Chapter 4), instant messaging (discussed in Chapter 5), and blogs and social media (discussed in Chapters 6 and 7).

Appropriate Use of the System

You should make sure employees know that their computers are company property, which the company may access at any time. In other words, the company has unfettered access to unfinished novels, vacation photos, spreadsheets of eBay sales, or any other private data that an employee saves to a company machine or hard drive. You should also require employees to limit their personal use of the computer system. The policy below spells out those limitations.

The Company may provide you with computer equipment and access to the Company's network in order to perform your job.

Use of Computer Equipment

The Company's computer equipment and network are intended for business use. You may use the Company's computer equipment for occasional personal purposes, but you may do so during nonwork hours only. Excessive personal use of the Company's computer equipment, even during nonwork hours, will be cause for discipline.

The Company has the ability to access and review all information stored on the Company's computer equipment and network. The Company reserves the right to perform such an inspection at any time, for any reason. You should not expect that any files, records, or other data stored on the Company's equipment and network will be private, even if you attempt to protect its privacy (for example, by using a password or designating it as "personal").

Lessons From the Real World

Employee's home computer can be searched.

Robert Zieminski was an executive at TBG Insurance Services Corporation. TBG gave him two computers to use for work: One sat on his desk at the office, and the other was at his home.

Zieminski signed a company policy regarding use of its electronic and telephone equipment, which said in part that he would use the computers for business purposes only, that he would not use the equipment for "improper, derogatory, defamatory, obscene, or other inappropriate purposes," and that improper use of the computers could result in discipline, including termination. He also agreed that the company could monitor his computer use "as needed," and that his computer communications were not private.

The company fired Zieminski, claiming that he had repeatedly accessed pornographic sites on the Internet from his work computer. Zieminski filed a wrongful termination lawsuit, alleging that the company really fired him because a large portion of his stock in the company was about to vest; he also said that he never intentionally accessed porn sites, but instead that those sites simply "popped up" on his computer screen.

As part of the lawsuit, TBG asked Zieminski to hand over his home computer. Zieminski agreed to give back the computer, but insisted that he had to delete or destroy some personal information on the computer, which he contended was protected by his right to privacy. Zieminski claimed that, despite the monitoring policy he signed, employees understood that they could use their home computers for personal purposes, and that his computer included tax returns, personal correspondence, and records created by his wife and children. TBG countered that it had to see the computer intact in order to find out whether he accessed the same pornographic sites from home, which would tend to undermine his claim that those sites popped up on his work computer involuntarily.

Lessons From the Real World (continued)

The California Court of Appeals sided with TBG and required Zieminski to hand over the computer without deleting anything. TBG's policy put Zieminski on notice that his computer use could be monitored, and Zieminski signed that policy. Therefore, he could not argue that he had any reasonable expectation of privacy in the contents of his computer, even though it was in his home and was used by his family members.

TBG Insurance Service Corp v. Superior Court of Los Angeles County, 96 Cal.App.4th 4443 (Cal. App. 2nd District, 2002).

CAUTION

If you find child pornography on company computers, you may have a duty to report it. According to the National Conference of State Legislatures (www.ncsl.org), at least ten states require computer technicians or ISPs to report child pornography they find in the course of their work. These laws don't require monitoring or searching for illegal material, but it must be reported if found. Employers in other states may also have to notify authorities of child pornography, if they are mandatory reporters of child abuse under state law. If a company audit or monitoring turns up child pornography or other illegal material on company equipment, talk to a lawyer to find out how to proceed.

Remote Access to the Company's Computer System

If your company's employees work from home or at distant locations, you may have set up a virtual private network or other system by which these employees can access the company's servers. These systems can save significant time and money, as they allow employees to get the files and programs they need—and work collaboratively—from a distance. They also allow the company's technical support staff to access remote employee computers and help resolve problems from afar.

These systems typically have strong security features to ensure that only authorized users can get into the company's electronic business. So, if your company has invested the resources to get one of these systems, you undoubtedly want employees to use it. And, whether or not your company provides remote access, you probably don't want employees taking it upon themselves to download commercial software (or use online programs) that allow them into the company's network through a back door.

If your company has a virtual private network or other system, the last sentence of the second paragraph in the policy below should tell employees how (and whom) to ask to have it installed on their remote computers. If not, simply delete this paragraph.

The policy below also bans commercial file sharing or cloud storage services. These services allow employees to upload files to a virtual container, hosted on the provider's servers, which can then be accessed remotely. If your company uses an enterprise file sharing or cloud storage service, you can adapt the policy to specifically allow employees to use the corporate system you have chosen; the intent of the policy is to prohibit employees from using commercial or personal services, which may not have the security features of a model designed for business use.

Some employers choose to allow employees to use their personal smartphones or tablets for work purposes. If you go this route, often called "BYOD" (bring your own device), and you want to give employees remote access not just to email and calendaring applications, but also to files and documents, you'll need a secure delivery and storage system. But you won't want employees storing your company's information on servers and services over which you have no control. (For more on BYOD policies, see Chapter 9.)

Remote Access

While software and programs that allow users remote access to a computer (for example, access to your home computer from work or your work computer from home) can be convenient, they also present security risks. Therefore, employees are prohibited from using these tools to access their work computers (and the Company's servers and network) from a distance, or to access any outside computer from their work computers, unless specifically authorized by [*name of department that handles technical matters, such as "the IT department"*].

If you need remote access to your work computer from home or another distant location, please ask [*name of department that handles technical matters, such as "the IT department"*] to assist you in loading the appropriate tools and configuring them properly.

Employees are prohibited from using file hosting services or cloud storage services, such as Dropbox or Google Drive, for work-related files, unless specifically authorized by [*name of department that handles technical matters, such as "the IT department"*].

Remote Access Hack Leads to Lawsuits

After a number of restaurants faced hacking incidents in which customers' credit card information was stolen electronically, they sued the maker of their POS computer systems (Radiant Systems) and the reseller (Computer World). According to news reports, Computer World installed remote access software in the systems, to allow technicians to troubleshoot technical difficulties remotely. Unfortunately, the remote access channel for all of the systems was protected by the same password: "computer." Given this level of security, it probably wasn't too difficult for the people who hacked the system (and used stolen credit cards for $1.2 million in purchases).

Encryption and Encoding

Some of your company's employees may need to encrypt or encode sensitive information, especially if it is leaving the building virtually (on the Internet) or physically (on a laptop or flash drive, for example). This is particularly true of employees who handle private customer or client data, medical records, and so on.

However, many employees have no business need to use encryption or encoding software. In that situation, the only real reason to use such software is to prevent their employer from reading their documents or email messages. It's wise to inform employees that encryption—except under the direction of the company—is prohibited. This policy reinforces the principle that employees should have no expectation of privacy in data on their computer (encrypted or otherwise); and that the company has the right to access all computer data all of the time. Further, prohibiting encryption lowers the possibility that company trade secrets, know-how, and data will disappear.

Encryption and Encoding

You may not encrypt or encode any files, data, or other information stored on the Company's computer equipment or network. If your job requires you to use encryption or encoding software, you may use it only for Company-related reasons and only with the permission of [*position authorized to allow encryption/encoding, such as "the IT director"*].

Software

Some employees mistakenly believe that the company's copy of Adobe InDesign is free for all to use, wherever and whenever they choose. In truth, the company does not own its copy of InDesign: It has purchased a license to use it, usually only on one machine. If the license is violated—by employees or by the employer—the owner of the software can seek damages, often far exceeding the cost of the license, and the company will be on the hook.

Another big problem is software downloads from the Internet. Even if the download is legal (and many aren't; there are plenty of sites offering pirated software), it may well create a security risk for your company. Software downloads may include viruses and other malware that can infect your company's whole system. Typically, the employee isn't even aware of these risks because the download is disguised as a legitimate software program.

To avoid these problems, your software policy should ban copying, installing, and downloading software without permission.

Software Use

It is our Company's policy to use licensed software only in accordance with the terms of its license agreement. Violating a license agreement is not only unethical; it is also illegal and can subject the Company to criminal prosecution and substantial monetary penalties.

To help us adhere to this policy, employees may not do any of the following without permission from [*position authorized to approve software use, such as "the IT director"*]:

- Copy any Company software program for any reason.

- Install a Company software program on any computer (including your home computer).

- Install a software program (including software licensed or owned by the employee) on any Company computer.

- Download any software program from the Internet to a Company computer.

The Company may audit Company-issued computers at any time to ensure compliance with this policy.

Lessons From the Real World

Company pays $500,000 to settle software piracy lawsuit.

The Software & Information Industry Association (SIIA), a trade organization for the software and digital content industry, has been very active in pursuing those who pirate its members' products. It goes after not only those who sell illegal copies of software, but also those who use them, including companies that unwittingly violate their licensing agreements.

In January 2008, the SIIA settled a lawsuit against Whittiker Legal Publishing Corporation. The suit claimed that Whittiker had installed and used copies of software made by SIIA member companies (including Adobe, Filemaker, and Symantec) without the proper licenses. Whittiker agreed to pay half a million dollars, destroy the unlicensed software, purchase replacement software, and adopt comprehensive software management policies. Even though the company used a third-party vendor to manage its software needs, Whittiker bore the ultimate legal responsibility for compliance.

Although it isn't clear how SIIA learned of Whittiker's license violations, many of its enforcement actions stem from whistleblowers. The SIIA has an antipiracy program that encourages people to report corporate misuse of software, offering rewards of up to one million dollars to those whose tips pan out. You can learn more at the SIIA's website, www.siia.net (select "IP Protection (IPP)").

CAUTION

Don't forget the acknowledgment form. If your company adopts the computer and software policy covered in this chapter, make sure you require employees to sign an acknowledgment form. You'll find an acknowledgment form and instructions at this book's online companion page; see the appendix for information on accessing the page.

Putting It All Together:
Sample Computer and Software Use Policy

Here's a sample policy for computer and software use adopted by a publishing company. Employees use their computers and software all the time, and the company wants to make sure that it doesn't violate its software licensing agreements. The company uses VPN software to allow employees remote access to the company's servers.

Sample Computer and Software Use Policy

The Company may provide you with computer equipment and access to the Company's network in order to perform your job.

Use of Computer Equipment

The Company's computer equipment and network are intended for business use. You may use the Company's computer equipment for occasional personal purposes, but you may do so during nonwork hours only. Excessive personal use of the Company's computer equipment, even during nonwork hours, will be cause for discipline.

The Company has the ability to access and review all information stored on the Company's computer equipment and network. The Company reserves the right to perform such an inspection at any time, for any reason. You should not expect that any files, records, or other data stored on the Company's equipment and network will be private, even if you attempt to protect its privacy (for example, by using a password or designating it as "personal").

Remote Access

While software and programs that allow users remote access to a computer (for example, access to your home computer from work or your work computer from home) can be convenient, they also present security risks. Therefore, employees are prohibited from using these tools to access their work computers (and the Company's servers and network) from a distance, or to access any outside computer from their work computers, unless specifically authorized by the IT director.

If you need remote access to your work computer from home or another distant location, please ask the IT director to assist you in loading the appropriate tools and configuring them properly.

Employees are prohibited from using file hosting services or cloud storage services, such as Dropbox or Google Drive for work-related files, unless specifically authorized by the IT director.

Sample Computer and Software Use Policy (continued)

Encryption and Encoding

You may not encrypt or encode any files, data, or other information stored on the Company's computer equipment or network. If your job requires you to use encryption or encoding software, you may use it only for Company-related reasons and only with the permission of the IT director.

Software Use

It is our Company's policy to use licensed software only in accordance with the terms of its license agreement. Violating a license agreement is not only unethical; it is also illegal and can subject the Company to criminal prosecution and substantial monetary penalties.

To help us adhere to this policy, employees may not do any of the following without permission from the IT director:

- Copy any Company software program for any reason.

- Install a Company software program on any computer (including your home computer).

- Install a software program (including software licensed or owned by the employee) on any Company computer.

- Download any software program from the Internet to a Company computer.

The Company may audit Company-issued computers at any time to ensure compliance with this policy.

Email

In This Chapter:

Policy Provisions for Email

☐ Use of the Email System

☐ Email Is Not Private

    ☐ Optional Policy Language for Monitoring That Flags Keywords

    ☐ Optional Policy Language for Random Monitoring

    ☐ Optional Policy Language for "Keylogger" Monitoring

☐ All Conduct Rules Apply to Email

☐ Guidelines for Email Writing

☐ Email Security

☐ Retaining and Deleting Email Messages

Perhaps more than any innovation covered in this book, email has revolutionized the way we work. Email can be terrifically efficient. It allows us to communicate quickly, send each other documents, work offsite, work in teams that are geographically dispersed, and document negotiations and decisions, all at warp speed.

But email also has its dark side. Every email message creates an electronic record—in effect, a document that a company might have to hand over in a lawsuit. In addition, the apparent informality of email encourages behavior that people might not engage in face to face, like "flaming," circulating inappropriate jokes, or sharing confidential information. And the speed and virtuality of email also make it easier to commit all manner of workplace misconduct, from harassment to trade secret theft.

Email Bankruptcy

According to the Radicati Group, the typical corporate employee who used email in 2015 sent 34 messages and received 88 messages (76 of them legitimate) every day. Unfortunately, this number is well above the 50 emails per day a 2010 Harris Interactive survey showed to be the "magic number," beyond which employees start to feel like they can't keep up. One of the results of this discrepancy: A 2009 survey in the United Kingdom revealed that almost ¾ of employees spend at least an hour each day dealing with email, and that the average employee inbox includes 2,769 saved messages!

Given the size of the pileup, it's no wonder that some overwhelmed users resort to "email bankruptcy": deleting the entire contents of one's inbox to get a fresh start.

If you're having trouble believing that email can cause this much trouble, consider these statistics:
- Almost half of employees have sent or received emails that include jokes, stories, or pictures of a "questionable" nature (that is, with racy or sexual content, or that are politically incorrect). (2005 Harris Interactive Poll for Fortiva.)

- Six percent of employees have emailed confidential company information to someone they shouldn't have. (Gregg Keizer, "Email Spills Corporate Secrets," *InformationWeek*, December 12, 2005.)
- Although 92% of employees surveyed said that they had never sent an email that put their company at risk, 68% in fact had. (2005 Harris Interactive Poll for Fortiva.)
- More than a quarter of companies in a recent survey have fired an employee for email misuse; most of those terminations were for inappropriate or offensive language and violation of company rules. (2007 Electronic Monitoring & Surveillance Survey, conducted by the American Management Association and The ePolicy Institute.)
- Fifteen percent of companies have faced a lawsuit triggered by employee email, and almost one quarter of companies have had their email subpoenaed by courts and regulators. (2006 Electronic Monitoring & Surveillance Survey, conducted by the American Management Association and The ePolicy Institute.)

To reap the considerable benefits of email while keeping risks to a minimum, your company must adopt a sensible and comprehensive email policy and require employees to sign off on it. This chapter explains everything you'll need to cover, including personal use of email, email monitoring, archiving and retention of messages, rules on appropriate content, and more.

"Reply All" Annoys Most

A 2013 survey by CPP, the company that publishes the Myers-Briggs personality test (among other things), revealed that email is the workplace communication tool most likely to lead to confusion and resentment. Why? Among email recipients, the biggest offender was overuse of "reply all." Runners-up in the unpopularity contest included messages that are vague or confusing, too long, contained too much "chitchat," or used bad grammar.

RELATED TOPIC

Information on personal Web-based accounts. This chapter covers only the company's own email system. However, some employees use their company's Internet connection (or use handheld devices such as iPhones) to send and receive email on their own personal accounts (for example, Gmail or Yahoo!). You can find more information on this issue in Chapter 4.

Personal Use of Email System

In the first part of your email policy, you should explain your company's policy on using the company's equipment to send personal email messages, such as messages to friends and family members, or messages to coworkers about nonwork topics, such as sports, politics, or parties. The most practical approach—and currently the safest, from a legal perspective—is to allow some personal use, with restrictions.

Prohibiting All Personal Use

Some companies don't want employees to use their email systems for personal messages, period. After all, the equipment belongs to the company, personal messages take employees away from their work and create potential liabilities, and then there's the storage and bandwidth problem. So why not just ban all personal use?

One major problem with an outright ban on personal use of business email is that everyone will break the rule. Even in our wired world, in which there are alternate ways to communicate instantly (like personal email accounts and smartphones), many people still send occasional personal messages from a corporate account. Perhaps someone wants to invite work colleagues to a social event, needs to send a quick personal note without opening a personal email account (and getting bogged down in the messages accumulating there), or simply would rather type at a keyboard than on a phone screen. Regardless of the reason, a policy forbidding any personal use of email will probably be violated regularly by most of your company's employees.

Because these policies are so often violated, they are seldom enforced, at least not consistently. Companies rarely have the time and energy to spend monitoring every transmission, then imposing discipline on everyone who sends a personal message. Instead, companies enforce the policy when an employee crosses the line by spending significant work time on personal messages, sending large attachments, sending messages that include racial jokes or sexual material, and so on. It's much easier—and safer, from a legal standpoint—to ban these types of misconduct rather than any and all personal use.

Any time an employer enforces a policy inconsistently, it takes a legal risk. An employee who is disciplined for violating the policy when others are not could point to that inconsistency as evidence of an illegal motive, such as discrimination or retaliation.

> **EXAMPLE:** Carla complains that her manager, Jim, has been sending her sexually explicit jokes on the company's email system. The company has a policy that prohibits all personal email, but it doesn't monitor employee email and has yet to enforce the policy.
>
> The company begins its investigation by reviewing Carla's and Jim's email accounts. The investigator discovers Jim's harassing messages, but also discovers that Carla occasionally uses the company's email system for family matters, including corresponding with her children's teachers and coaches. The company gives Jim a written warning for misconduct; Carla receives a written warning for violating the company's email policy. Because Carla already has a written warning for performance problems, she is now ineligible for raises and promotions for a year.
>
> Several weeks later, the company receives a demand letter from Carla's attorney. The claim? That the company retaliated against Carla for complaining of sexual harassment. The letter states that other employees routinely used the email system for personal matters, but Carla was the only one disciplined, and only after she complained of possible sexual harassment. The company's attorney advises it to rescind Carla's written warning immediately and perhaps even consider a small monetary settlement. Even though Carla violated the policy, it looks too much like retaliation to enforce it for the first time against someone who had just raised concerns about harassment.

Inconsistent enforcement based on the content of the message could lead to legal problems as well. For example, if your company bans all personal messages but typically looks the other way when employees send them, it could face a discrimination claim if it disciplines an employee for sending out a message proselytizing for his or her religion or publicizing an upcoming event that has a particular ethnic or racial focus, such as a Cinco de Mayo parade or a conference for African American entrepreneurs.

Your company could even face an unfair labor practices charge if its policy prohibits all nonwork use of email. The National Labor Relations Board (NLRB), the federal agency that enforces the laws relating to unions and employee organizing, has recently held that employers may not prohibit employees from using company email, during nonwork hours, to communicate about wages, hours, working conditions, and union-related issues. The NLRB has said that an employer may have a policy limiting use of its email to business purposes only if such a rule is consistently enforced and is necessary to maintain productivity or discipline (a situation that the NLRB believes will rarely apply). This decision is currently making its way through the review process, so the issue may ultimately be decided differently in the federal courts. For the time being, however, employers who ban all personal use of email are treading on very thin legal ice.

For all of these reasons, policies that ban all personal use are impractical and invite legal exposure.

Allowing Some Personal Use

To balance the company's interest in preventing employees from engaging in personal pursuits while they are supposed to be working against employees' desire to send occasional personal messages, consider policy language that allows some personal use. The policy provision below allows employees to send personal messages, but only outside of work hours.

You can (and should) further limit the types of messages employees may send and put them on notice that using email for harassment, or to transmit confidential information will lead to discipline (see "Content Rules," below).

Use of the Email System

The email system is intended for official Company business. Although you may use the email system occasionally for personal messages, you may do so during nonworking hours only.

Privacy

Your email policy absolutely must inform employees that their messages are not private and must reserve the company's right to monitor and read messages at any time. Even if your company has no plans to actively monitor employee email, it may one day have to do so if an employee is accused of sending sexually harassing messages, transmitting trade secrets to a competitor, or using email to spread false rumors about another employee, for example.

You might be wondering why your company has to tell employees that it might read email messages that are sent on company equipment, especially if those messages might get the company in legal trouble. The answer lies in the way privacy law works. As applied to workplace issues, privacy law generally balances an employee's reasonable expectations of privacy against the employer's reasons for monitoring, searching, and so on. The more a company can do to diminish employee expectations of privacy, the more legal protection it has when monitoring employee communications. And one of the best ways to do this is by explicitly stating, in a written policy, that email messages are not private.

> **Email Is Not Private**
>
> Email messages, including attachments, sent and received on Company equipment are the property of the Company. We reserve the right to access, monitor, read, and/or copy email messages at any time, for any reason. You should not expect privacy for any email you send using Company equipment, including messages that you consider to be personal, or label with a designation such as "Personal" or "Private."

Monitoring

If your company has monitoring software it plans to use, or if someone will be assigned to read employee email on a regular basis, you should let employees know in your written policy. After all, the purpose of an email policy is not only to allow the company to read those problematic messages after they've been sent, but also to deter employees from sending them in the first place. Telling employees that their messages will be monitored and/or read will almost certainly help accomplish this second goal.

CAUTION

Choose your monitors wisely. Before your company gives anyone unfettered access to their coworkers' email, it should consider this: According to a 2007 survey, one-third of IT administrators admit snooping through employee email, files, and other confidential information. (Manek Dubash, "Study: IT Admins Read Private Email," *PC World*, May 29, 2007.) These employees apparently had very little "need to know," but the opportunity to spy on their coworkers was just too tempting. If you choose to monitor, select your readers with great care and check up to make sure that they aren't overstepping their authority.

Lessons From the Real World

Is an employee's email to an attorney confidential?

One of the bedrock principles of the law is the attorney-client privilege, which protects the confidentiality of conversations between lawyers and their clients. In the past, employers had very few ways to get their hands on communications between an employee and a lawyer, which were likely to occur in person or by letter or personal phone call.

Today, however, there are some (admittedly risk-taking) employees who use company email to correspond with a lawyer, often about suing the employer whose email system they're using. If the employer recovers those email messages, whether in the normal course of monitoring or as part of preparing to defend a lawsuit the employee later files, can it read them?

Courts have ruled different ways on this issue, depending on whether the employee used a personal or work account to send the messages and on the employer's policies and practices. For example, one New York court found that a doctor who sent email to his lawyer on his employer's system had waived the attorney-client privilege because the employer's policy prohibited personal use of the system and told employees that it monitored employee email. (*Scott v. Beth Israel Medical Center*, 847 N.Y.S. 3d 436 (N.Y. Sup. 2007).) On the other hand, several courts have found that an employee who uses a personal email account for legal correspondence, even if using a company computer, has not waived the privilege, regardless of the employer's monitoring practices and policies. (*Stengart v. Loving Care Agency Inc.*, 990 A.2d 650 (2010); *Curto v. Medical World Communications, Inc.*, 2006 WL 1318387 (E.D. N.Y. 2006).) The moral of the story? Just because you have the ability to read an employee's email messages to an attorney doesn't mean you have the legal right to do so: Speak to a lawyer yourself before proceeding.

Whether your company should regularly monitor employee email is a tough issue to sort through. Doing so will force employees to take the email policy seriously and thereby make them less likely to send messages that are harassing, threatening, or otherwise in violation of your policy. It's just human nature: We aren't as quick to break the rules if we think we will get caught.

But there are some serious downsides as well, with employee dissatisfaction topping the list. Employees don't want to feel like the company doesn't trust them or plans to check up on their every keystroke. Monitoring also costs time and money. And some employers just find monitoring distasteful. They don't want to be cast in the role of Big Brother.

Ultimately, the company's philosophy, workforce, and needs will determine whether the benefits of monitoring outweigh the disadvantages. If your company has no immediate plans to monitor or read employee email, you need not add additional monitoring language: The provision on privacy, above, is sufficient.

If, however, your company plans to regularly monitor messages, you should add that information to your policy immediately following the privacy provision, above. What your policy should say depends on how your monitoring software works. Here are some sample provisions:

Optional Policy Language for Monitoring That Flags Keywords

In addition, the Company's software automatically searches the messages you send for questionable content, including sexual or racial comments, threats, trade secrets, competitive information, and curse words. Any message deemed questionable will be forwarded to, and read by, Company management.

Optional Policy Language for Random Monitoring

In addition, the Company will select and read employee messages at random to ensure that employees are in compliance with this policy.

Optional Policy Language for "Keylogger" Monitoring

In addition, the Company's monitoring software automatically creates a copy of every message you draft, even if you never send it. Company personnel will regularly read these copies to make sure that no employee violates this policy.

CAUTION

Don't monitor selectively. The NLRB has said that employers who monitor employee email can get into trouble if they single out union activists for scrutiny, increase monitoring during an organizing campaign, or focus their monitoring on protected communications, such as discussions of wages, hours, and working conditions. As long as you follow your usual monitoring procedures consistently and regularly, however, you won't run afoul of this prohibition.

Lessons From the Real World

Employer might be liable for wrongful death when employee threatened his family via company email.

Christopher Coleman worked in a high-level security position at Joyce Meyer Ministries (JMM). In May 2009, his wife and two children were killed. Coleman was convicted of their murder.

In 2011, the administrator of the family's estates sued Coleman and his former employer for wrongful death. Among several legal theories, the administrator claimed that JMM was negligent in undertaking to protect the deceased family members from harm. Although the trial court in Illinois threw out this claim, the court of appeals reinstated the claim, finding that the employer could be held liable if the facts were as the administrator alleged.

The family had received death threats from a JMM computer from November 2008 through the murders. The complaint alleges that the employer knew about these threats and had promised to investigate pursuant to its electronic communications policy, to discipline anyone found to have violated that policy, to provide security for the family, and to notify law enforcement of these threats. The complaint stated that JMM did not do these things, and its failure to follow through led to the family's deaths.

Regions Bank v. Joyce Meyer Ministries, Inc., 15 N.E.3f 545 (2014).

Content Rules

Your policy should tell employees what types of messages are allowed and prohibited. It's also a good idea to remind employees what email is: an electronic record of a communication, which can be saved, printed, forwarded to unknown recipients, and otherwise leave the building.

Software Helps Companies Keep It Clean and Kind

The investment bank Goldman Sachs has become famous for more than a few things in the recent economic recession, including the foul language in employee email messages. After a Senator read some of them aloud at a Congressional hearing, Goldman decided to clean up its act. According to news reports in July 2010, Goldman now prohibits foul language in email, and enforces the rule with screening software.

But what about companies that are less concerned with outright cursing than with employee email messages that seem curt, unprofessional, or unkind? After all, email is a "cold" medium (one that requires the reader to fill in a lot of blanks, per the classic definition by Marshall McLuhan). This means there's lots of room for incorrect assumptions and misinterpretations.

The search for an electronic solution to this more subtle problem has led to the creation of ToneCheck, a software program that scans email messages for words and phrases that reflect the intensity of eight emotions, including humiliation, anger, and sadness. These instances are flagged with emoticons, giving the writer an opportunity to revise the message to avoid conveying unintended or unprofessional feelings along with the budget forecast or meeting agenda.

Harassment, Threats, and Other Misconduct

One of the most common email problems employers face is electronic harassment: sexually explicit content, lewd or racist jokes, and inappropriate stories or name calling via the company's email system. Your policy should make clear that all company policies relating to harassment and other misconduct apply equally to email.

All Conduct Rules Apply to Email

All of our policies and rules of conduct apply to employee use of the email system. This means, for example, that you may not use the email system to send harassing or discriminatory messages, including messages with explicit sexual content or pornographic images; to send threatening messages; or to reveal Company trade secrets.

Netiquette

Your company may want to include some writing guidelines in its policy, especially if you have a lot of entry-level or otherwise inexperienced employees. Because email is seen as informal, some employees send out even work-related messages sprinkled with emoticons and exclamation points, written in all lowercase or capital letters, or filled with acronyms or usages peculiar to the online world. Some employees also make the mistake of sending out email without considering its content or style, only later to regret having expressed anger too hastily or sending a message that doesn't look professional.

You can include as much or as little detail as you like about writing style. Here is a policy provision that includes a handful of common "netiquette" rules:

Guidelines for Email Writing

1. Always spell-check or proofread your business email messages. Email is official Company correspondence. Spelling errors in email are all too common, and they look sloppy and unprofessional.

2. Use lowercase and capital letters in the same way that you would in a letter. Using all capital letters is the email equivalent of shouting at someone; it can also be hard on the eyes. Failing to use capital letters at all (to begin a sentence or formal noun) can confuse readers and seem overly cute. Unless you are writing poetry, use standard capitalization.

3. Remember your audience. Although email encourages informal communication, that might not be the most appropriate style to use if you are addressing the CEO of an important customer. And, remember that your email can be forwarded to unintended recipients, some of whom may not appreciate joking comments or informalities.

4. Don't use email for confidential matters. Again, remember the unintended recipient. Your email might be forwarded to someone you didn't anticipate or might be sitting at a printer for all to see. If you need to have a confidential business discussion, do it in person or over the phone.

5. Send messages sparingly. There is rarely a need to copy everyone in the Company on an email. Carefully consider who really needs to see the message, and address it accordingly.

6. Don't leave the subject line blank. Always include a brief description, so readers will know what your email is about at a glance. This makes it easier for all of us to manage our email and makes it more likely that you will receive a response to your message.

7. Don't overuse the "urgent" tag. Mark a message as urgent only if it is truly important and must be answered right away.

CAUTION

Email policies requiring civility may be illegal. In the past couple of years, the NLRB has come down hard on employer communications policies that require employees to be professional, civil, appropriate, or otherwise mannerly in their speech. Such policies are seen as a potential brake on employees who want to talk to each other about their pay, work hours, benefits, and other working conditions. The National Labor Relations Act protects conversations on these topics, and employers may not interfere with employees' rights to have these discussions, whether or not the employees are represented by a union. In this rapidly changing area of law, employers would be wise to consult with a lawyer.

Whoops!

Have you ever misaddressed an email, sent an email without a promised attachment, or gotten an email that you considered inappropriate? Well, you're not alone. According to a 2007 *InformationWeek* survey of more than 700 employees:

- 15% said they'd received an email sent in anger.
- 13% said they'd gotten flirtatious email.
- 23% said they'd received email they considered politically incorrect.
- 20% had sent an email to the wrong person.
- Almost 40% had forgotten to include an attachment in an email they sent.
- A very sad 5% had received a humiliating message that was copied to others.

Anyone can make these mistakes or errors in judgment. Even those who really should know better, like, say, Microsoft, which accidentally sent a reporter an email message with a surprising attachment: an internal dossier its PR firm had compiled on the reporter. The reporter was writing a story on Microsoft's blogging initiative as evidence of the company's effort to be more transparent with the public. Ouch!

Viruses and Other Security Threats

Your policy should give employees a few tips to help them avoid launching a virus, Trojan horse, worm, or other electronic threat on your company's email system.

Email Security

To avoid email viruses and other threats, employees should not open email attachments or click on links in email from people and businesses they don't recognize, particularly if the email appears to have been forwarded multiple times or has a nonexistent or peculiar subject heading. Even if you know the sender, do not open an email attachment or click a link that has a strange name or is not referenced in the body of the email. It may have been transmitted automatically, without the sender's knowledge.

If you believe your computer has been infected by a virus, worm, or other security threat to the Company's system, you must inform the IT department immediately.

Employees may not share their email passwords with anyone, including coworkers or family members. Revealing passwords to the Company's email system could allow an outsider to access the Company's network.

Retention and Deletion

Email messages create electronic records. Your email policy must tell employees how to manage those records: that is, which records to keep and which to delete.

Email messages often include important company records that your company either should or is legally required to retain. For example, if applicants apply for a job by email, those email messages are hiring records that, like other hiring records, must be kept for three years. Of course, your company will also want to retain electronic contracts, agreements, records of negotiations, consent forms, and so on.

Lessons From the Real World

Destroying email messages can be very costly.

Laura Zubulake was an equities trader at UBS Warburg. After she was fired, she sued UBS for sex discrimination, failure to promote, and retaliation. During the lawsuit, she asked UBS to hand over email messages that she claimed included biased comments about her by UBS decision makers.

UBS protested that it would cost hundreds of thousands of dollars to retrieve and review its email messages to decide which it had to hand over. The court decided that UBS would have to hand over all relevant messages that were still readily available, but that Zubulake would have to pay part of the estimated cost of restoring backup tapes. Several orders later, it became apparent that some relevant email messages had been deleted after the lawsuit began, against the court's instructions.

The court found that these email messages had been destroyed willfully. As a result, the court ordered UBS to pay some of Zubulake's pretrial costs. More importantly, the court instructed the jury that UBS had destroyed the email messages, and that the jury could conclude that the messages would have been harmful to UBS's case. After hearing all of the evidence as well as this instruction about the missing emails, the jury awarded more than $29 million to Zubulake.

Zubulake v. UBS Warburg L.L.C., 229 F.R.D. 422 (S.D. N.Y. 2004); Eduardo Porter, "UBS Ordered to Pay $29 Million in Sex Bias Lawsuit," *The New York Times,* April 7, 2005.

On the other hand, the great majority of email messages sent and received by your company's employees can—and should—be deleted as soon as they are dealt with. Email messages take up a lot of virtual space, and employees who are email packrats can quickly overload your company's storage capacity.

What's more, your company can be required to produce email messages if it is sued, just as it has to hand over paper documents. The more messages your employees keep, the more messages your company will have to comb through—and possibly hand over—if it is faced with a lawsuit. The Federal Rules of Civil Procedure (FRCP), which set the ground rules for federal lawsuits, were recently amended to require parties to a lawsuit to hand over electronic evidence just like any other evidence, not only when the other party asks for it in discovery but also as part of their pretrial disclosures.

However, the FRCP also acknowledge that electronic evidence is different from regular paper documents, in that it may be difficult to access because it's been destroyed in the regular course of business. Many companies have a practice of deleting email messages and writing over backup tapes after a certain period of time. A company won't face sanctions or penalties for failing to hand over electronic evidence if that evidence was destroyed because of the routine, good-faith operation of an electronic information system. If, for example, your company's email program automatically purges email messages after a certain number of days and reuses its storage capacity by writing over older information, it won't face legal trouble if it can't hand over messages that were destroyed in the regular course of business.

This protection doesn't extend to evidence that's destroyed after the company knows that it is (or might soon be) facing a lawsuit, however. Once this happens, the company has a legal duty to preserve all evidence that might be relevant to the case, including email messages and other electronic information. (This is commonly referred to as a "litigation hold.") If your company faces litigation, it will have to immediately override its usual purge procedures and make sure it hangs on to every applicable document.

Lessons From the Real World

Employee can be fired for preserving confidential email messages by sending them to her personal account.

When Sarah Aldrich, an employee at Rural Health Services, grew concerned about her future at the company, she forwarded a number of email messages from the company's CEO, Linda Buck, to her own personal email account. Buck had sent some email regarding a former employee's age discrimination claims against the company; she had also sent messages instructing employees to go through their email and delete any references to the facts underlying the former employee's claims.

Aldrich forwarded all email Buck had sent her, without regard to their content. Some of the messages contained confidential patient information. When the company's IT administrator discovered Aldrich had forwarded the messages, he asked her to delete them all. Aldrich refused several times and was fired.

Among other things, Aldrich claimed that she was fired in retaliation for refusing to destroy evidence that might be relevant to her former coworker's discrimination claim. The federal Court of Appeals disagreed, however. Aldrich was not directly involved in her former coworker's lawsuit, and she was not forwarding the email in response to a request from a lawyer or a subpoena. Because the email messages contained private patient information, and because all employees were under strict instructions to maintain their confidentiality, the court found that Aldrich's decision to forward them in case they were later helpful in a lawsuit was not reasonable, under the circumstances.

Aldrich v. Rural Health Services Consortium, Case No. 14-5074 (6th Cir. 2014).

Retaining and Deleting Email Messages

Because email messages are electronic records, certain messages must be retained for compliance purposes. Please refer to our record-keeping policy for guidance on which records must be kept, and for how long. If you have any questions about whether and how to retain a particular email message, please ask your manager.

Because of the large volume of emails our Company sends and receives each day, we discourage employees from storing large numbers of email messages that are not subject to the retention rules explained above. Please make a regular practice of deleting email messages once you have read and/or responded to them. If you need to save a particular message, you may print out a paper copy, archive the email, or save it on your hard drive or disk. The Company will purge email messages that have not been archived after _____ days.

The Company may have occasion to suspend our usual rules about deleting email messages (for example, if the Company is involved in a lawsuit requiring it to preserve evidence). If this happens, employees will be notified of the procedures to follow to save email messages. Failing to comply with such a notice could subject the Company to serious legal consequences, and will result in discipline, up to and including termination.

CAUTION

Don't forget the acknowledgment form. If your company adopts the email policy covered in this chapter, make sure you require employees to sign an acknowledgment form. You'll find a sample acknowledgment form and instructions at this book's online companion page; see the appendix for instructions on accessing the page.

Putting It All Together: Sample Email Policy

Here's a sample email policy for a large financial services company. The company has had some problems with employees sending inappropriate email messages in the past, so it uses software that monitors keywords. It also prohibits all forms of employee solicitation, even for charitable causes. Because many of its employees are relatively new to the work world, the company has decided to adopt the netiquette guidelines as well.

Sample Email Policy

Use of the Email System

The email system is intended for official Company business. Although you may use the email system occasionally for personal messages, you may do so during nonworking hours only.

Email Is Not Private

Email messages, including attachments, sent and received on Company equipment are the property of the Company. We reserve the right to access, monitor, read, and/or copy email messages at any time, for any reason. You should not expect privacy for any email you send using Company equipment, including messages that you consider to be personal, or label with a designation such as "Personal" or "Private."

In addition, the Company's software automatically searches the messages you send for questionable content, including sexual or racial comments, threats, trade secrets, competitive information, and curse words. Any message deemed questionable will be forwarded to, and read by, Company management.

All Conduct Rules Apply to Email

All of our policies and rules of conduct apply to employee use of the email system. This means, for example, that you may not use the email system to send harassing or discriminatory messages, including messages with explicit sexual content or pornographic images; to send threatening messages; or to reveal Company trade secrets.

Guidelines for Email Writing

1. Always spell-check or proofread your business email messages. Email is official Company correspondence. Spelling errors in email are all too common, and they look sloppy and unprofessional.

2. Use lowercase and capital letters in the same way that you would in a letter. Using all capital letters is the email equivalent of shouting at

Sample Email Policy (continued)

someone; it can also be hard on the eyes. Failing to use capital letters at all (to begin a sentence or formal noun) can confuse readers and seem overly cute. Unless you are writing poetry, use standard capitalization.

3. Remember your audience. Although email encourages informal communication, that might not be the most appropriate style to use if you are addressing the CEO or an important customer. And, remember that your email can be forwarded to unintended recipients, some of whom may not appreciate joking comments or informalities.

4. Don't use email for confidential matters. Again, remember the unintended recipient. Your email might be forwarded to someone you didn't anticipate or might be sitting at a printer for all to see. If you need to have a confidential business discussion, do it in person or over the phone.

5. Send messages sparingly. There is rarely a need to copy everyone in the Company on an email. Carefully consider who really needs to see the message, and address it accordingly.

6. Don't leave the subject line blank. Always include a brief description, so readers will know what your email is about at a glance. This makes it easier for all of us to manage our email and makes it more likely that you will receive a response to your message.

7. Don't overuse the "urgent" tag. Mark a message as urgent only if it is truly important and must be answered right away.

Email Security

To avoid email viruses and other threats, employees should not open email attachments or click on links in email from people and businesses they don't recognize, particularly if the email appears to have been forwarded multiple times or has a nonexistent or peculiar subject heading. Even if you know the sender, do not open an email attachment or click a link that has a strange name or is not referenced in the body of the email. It may have been transmitted automatically, without the sender's knowledge.

Sample Email Policy (continued)

If you believe your computer has been infected by a virus, worm, or other security threat to the Company's system, you must inform the IT department immediately.

Employees may not share their email passwords with anyone, including coworkers or family members. Revealing passwords to the Company's email system could allow an outsider to access the Company's network.

Retaining and Deleting Email Messages

Because email messages are electronic records, certain messages must be retained for compliance purposes. Please refer to our record-keeping policy for guidance on which records must be kept, and for how long. If you have any questions about whether and how to retain a particular email message, please ask your manager.

Because of the large volume of emails our Company sends and receives each day, we discourage employees from storing large numbers of email messages that are not subject to the retention rules explained above. Please make a regular practice of deleting email messages once you have read and/or responded to them. If you need to save a particular message, you may print out a paper copy, archive the email, or save it on your hard drive or disk. The Company will purge email messages that have not been archived after 90 days.

The Company may have occasion to suspend our usual rules about deleting email messages (for example, if the Company is involved in a lawsuit requiring it to preserve evidence). If this happens, employees will be notified of the procedures to follow to save email messages. Failing to comply with such a notice could subject the Company to serious legal consequences, and will result in discipline, up to and including termination.

Internet Use

In This Chapter:

Policy Provisions for Employee Internet Use

☐ Personal Use of the Internet

☐ Prohibited Uses of the Internet

☐ No Personal Posts Using Company Equipment

Internet Use Is Not Private:

    ☐ Alternative 1: Privacy Policy Reserving the Right to Monitor

    ☐ Alternative 2: Privacy Policy for Companies That Monitor Regularly

☐ Don't Use Personal Email Accounts for Work

Access to Personal Email Accounts:

    ☐ Alternative 1: No Access to Personal Email Accounts

    ☐ Alternative 2: Rules for Accessing Personal Email Accounts

    ☐ Optional Policy Language for Blocking Access to Personal Email

    ☐ Optional Policy Language for Keylogger Software

t's no wonder that many of us have become blasé about the Internet. It is so ubiquitous, so useful, and so essential to our work that it's hard to believe that we once had to manually track shipments, book travel, locate information, map a trip, go shopping, or conduct research without it.

As most businesses are aware, however, allowing employees unlimited Internet access poses problems and threats. As a virtual gateway in and out of the company, the Internet tempts employees to spend work time on personal pursuits like bargain hunting, checking sports scores, joining chat rooms, checking their personal email account or social networking pages, and even looking for a new job. In addition, employees can use the Internet to access inappropriate material—for example pornography, gambling, and hate speech—which is often deemed offensive by coworkers.

Where Employees Go Online

According to a 2006 survey by Websense, more than 60% of employees admitted to visiting personal websites at work, for an average of slightly more than three hours total per week. What types of sites did they visit? The most frequented nonwork sites were map sites, followed by news sites and weather sites. Banking, travel, and shopping sites were close behind.

Of course, a lot has changed on the Internet since 2006, the year Twitter was launched and only a couple of years after Facebook had been created in a dorm room. A 2012 survey by salary.com revealed that Facebook was by far the most popular personal site accessed at work, followed by LinkedIn. Remember MySpace? Neither did anyone who took the survey, but Pinterest and Twitter also made the top ten list.

Employee access to the Web can also inadvertently result in damage to the company's computer system and software, from viruses, spyware, and so on. In fact, experts say that more system attacks are launched on companies today via employee Internet surfing than through email.

Finally, the Internet provides a back door by which employees can send information out of the company, whether by transmitting company information through personal email or posting personal comments to outside sites, which can then be traced back to your company.

Do We Have Al Gore to Thank?

Most of the innovations discussed in this book rely on the Internet, known in previous incarnations as the World Wide Web or the Information Superhighway. And we all know who invented the Internet ... or do we?

In the run-up to the 2000 election, Al Gore was said to have claimed that he invented the Internet. But it turns out (1) he never said that, and (2) he wouldn't have been too far wrong if he did.

What Gore actually said, in answering a question from CNN's Wolf Blitzer as to why American voters should choose him over his primary competitor Bill Bradley, was that he "took the initiative in creating the Internet." And so he did: Among many other things, he drafted and sponsored the High Performance Communication and Computing Act of 1991, which led to the National Information Infrastructure and the development of Mosaic, a Web browser many believe to have begun the Internet boom of the 1990s.

Gore later made fun of his statement on *Late Night with David Letterman*, giving as number nine of his top ten list of rejected Gore-Lieberman campaign slogans, "Remember, America, I gave you the Internet and I can take it away!"

Personal Use of the Internet

Banning all personal use of the Internet leads to the same problems—employee resentment, selective enforcement, and so on—as banning all personal email. (See Chapter 3 for more information.) A more sensible approach is to allow limited personal use of the Internet during lunch, breaks, or other nonwork hours, as long as that use is not excessive and does not violate the policy's other prohibitions (see "Prohibited Uses of the Internet," below). This will help you not only avoid the problems that an outright ban can create, but also ensure that employees spent more of their work hours doing what your company is actually paying them to do, rather than shopping on Amazon, checking their Facebook page, or keeping tabs on their favorite sports teams.

After Black Friday Comes Cyber Monday

The day after Thanksgiving has been called "Black Friday," a reference to either the heavy traffic (and ensuing headaches) or the bottom-line profit associated with the biggest shopping day of the year. Those who prefer to shop online apparently do so on "Cyber Monday," the first business day after Thanksgiving, when employees return to their workplace computer terminals.

How much shopping do employees do? Challenger, Gray, and Christmas (an outplacement firm—and yes, that is their real name) estimated that more than 71 million employees would do some holiday shopping online on Cyber Monday, 2015. If each of those employees spent only 15 minutes shopping, it could cost companies almost $450 million in lost productivity.

And if those 12 minutes stretched into two full days? According to a survey conducted by the nonprofit ISACA, half of the employees surveyed planned to shop online from work in November and December 2009. On average, employees planned to spend more than 14 hours shopping online, from work, during this time period. The same survey found that one in ten employees who has a mobile work device planned to use it for holiday shopping.

> **Personal Use of the Internet**
>
> Our network and Internet access are for official Company business. Employees may access the Internet for personal use only outside of work hours and only in accordance with the other terms of this policy. An employee who engages in excessive Internet use, even during nonwork hours, may be subject to discipline.

Prohibited Uses of the Internet

Your policy should tell employees what types of Internet activities and sites are forbidden, what types of downloads and streaming activities are prohibited, and what restrictions the company places on employee postings to other sites.

Prohibited Sites and Downloads

Start by listing the types of electronic information that employees may not access from work. In addition to banning sites with offensive material (such as pornography and violent images), you should ban two types of downloads: those that violate the law—such as inappropriate use of copyrighted material, stolen music files, unlicensed software programs—or those that could infect your company's system—for example, files that may contain viruses or other system threats.

In addition, your company must also consider its tech capacity limits. Streaming audio or video—for example, listening to Internet radio stations or watching live sport events—can quickly overload your company's systems. If that's the case at your company, you'll want to add language banning these uses in your policy.

If your company blocks employee access to particular sites or types of sites using a technological solution—for example, filtering software—you should let employees know that their ability to access a site doesn't necessarily mean it's appropriate for viewing. (If your company doesn't use blocking software, simply delete the last paragraph of this section.)

Prohibited Uses of the Internet

Employees may not, at any time, access the Internet using Company equipment for any of the following purposes:

- To view websites that offer pornography, gambling, or violent imagery, or are otherwise inappropriate in the workplace.

- To operate an outside business, online auction, or other sales site; solicit money for personal purposes; or otherwise act for personal financial gain or profit.

- To download or copy software, games, text, photos, or any other works in violation of copyright, trademark, or other laws.

- To stream, run, or download any non–Company-licensed software program without the express consent of the IT department.

- To stream, run, or download music, video, games, widgets, or any form of multimedia, from the Internet.

- To read, open, or download any file from the Internet without first screening that file for viruses using the Company's virus detection software.

If you believe that your job may require you to do something that would otherwise be forbidden by this policy, ask your manager how to proceed.

To ensure that employees comply with this policy, we use software that will block your access to many prohibited sites. However, some inappropriate websites may escape detection by the software: The fact that you can access a particular site does not necessarily mean that site is appropriate for workplace viewing.

Lessons From the Real World

Is Internet sex addiction a disability?

James Pacenza worked for IBM for 19 years until he was fired after a coworker witnessed a chat room discussion about sex on Pacenza's computer screen. Pacenza claimed that his termination was illegal because, among other things, he visited Internet chat rooms as a way to "self-medicate" his disability.

Pacenza, a veteran of the Vietnam War, suffered from post-traumatic stress disorder and depression. Pacenza claimed that IBM shouldn't have fired him because Internet sex addiction was a manifestation of his disability. Therefore, the company's decision to fire him—rather than working with him to come up with a reasonable accommodation—was discriminatory.

Not surprisingly, IBM contended that Pacenza was fired for violating its policy on Internet misuse, and that it had no obligation to accommodate his desire to engage in sexual chat room discussions.

Pacenza lost his case, but the question of Internet addiction as a disability lingers on, whether the claimed addiction is to the Internet itself (for someone who can't be offline for more than a few hours or can't stop checking email) or to the Internet's ability to bring other addictive material directly to the user (for example, porn sites for a sex addict or gaming sites for a gambling addict). But that probably won't last forever. Today, you can find therapists who specialize in treating Internet addiction, scholarly articles on the problem, and even 12-step programs to combat the addiction (ironically, some are available online). And, "Internet Use Disorder," is recommended for further study in the DSM-5, the definitive guide to mental disorders used by mental health professionals.

Even if Internet sex addiction becomes a legally recognized disability, however, employers who utilize blocking software have little to worry about: One proposed "reasonable accommodation" is to make sure that employees can't access inappropriate sites—particularly porn sites—while at work, which is exactly what blocking software is designed to accomplish.

Prohibited Posts to Other Sites

When employees state their personal opinions by, for example, posting a comment to a blog or forum, those opinions could mistakenly be attributed to their employer (for example, if the employee or the employee's email address gives it away). In addition, any transmission may be traceable back to your company computers (or to an Internet Protocol address, a unique number that points to your company as a source).

At the same time, employees who post anything about your company's products absolutely must identify themselves and their employment relationship to your company. Rules adopted by the Federal Trade Commission in 2009 require any endorser of a product—including those who post online reviews or discuss products on online discussion boards—to reveal their relationship to the product's maker, if applicable. This includes employees who post content online about the things your company sells. Chapter 6 includes policy language to deal with this issue; you needn't include it here because this policy prohibits all personal posts using company equipment, period.

Your policy should prohibit employees from posting to other sites using company equipment. (For information on employee posts from personal computers to blogs, websites, or third-party sites, see Chapter 6.) Some of your company's employees might post online as part of their jobs. For example, a publicist or social media specialist might routinely post to other sites in their official capacities as employees. If your company has positions like these, you might want to add a sentence to the end of this part of the policy, such as "If you believe your job requires you to post online in your official capacity as a company employee, please speak to your supervisor."

No Personal Posts Using Company Equipment

Employees may not use the Company's equipment to transmit their personal opinions by, for example, posting a comment to a blog or contributing to an online forum. Even if you don't identify yourself as a Company employee, your use of Company equipment could cause your opinion to be mistaken for the Company's view.

Privacy

Just as you did in your email policy, you should tell employees that their Internet use is not private. A policy like this—whether you currently monitor employee Internet usage or just want to reserve the right in the future—may greatly minimize your company's legal exposure.

Here are some examples of situations when you might need to investigate an employee's Internet activity:

- Several employees complain that their manager is viewing pornography on his computer terminal. They claim that the manager has offensive pictures up on his screen when he calls them into his office for meetings or conversations. The manager denies everything.

- Posts to several online investor forums indicate that a publicly traded company will soon release a new product, resulting in a quick jump in its stock price. A few members of the company's management team sell off much of their stock shortly before the rumor is shown to be false.

- An employee's performance has declined significantly, and coworkers claim that he spends most of his time on Facebook. The employee claims that his job requires him to check social networking sites to see what job applicants have posted about themselves, but he doesn't access those sites from work for personal reasons.

If your company uses monitoring software (according to surveys, nearly ¾ of employers do), you should let employees know. After all, the goal is not just to keep track of where employees go on the Internet, but to stop them from going to inappropriate sites in the first place. Telling employees that they're being watched is sure to cut down on prohibited, unnecessary, and unauthorized surfing.

The first policy, below, simply reserves the right to monitor. The second version tells employees that monitoring is underway.

Alternative 1: Privacy Policy Reserving the Right to Monitor

Internet Use Is Not Private

We reserve the right to monitor employee use of the Internet at any time. You should not expect that your use of the Internet—including but not limited to the sites you visit, the amount of time you spend online, and the communications you have—will be private.

Alternative 2: Privacy Policy for Companies That Monitor Regularly

Internet Use Is Not Private

Our Company uses monitoring software that, among other things, tracks the sites an employee visits and how much time is spent at a particular site. You should not expect that your use of the Internet— including but not limited to the sites you visit, the amount of time you spend online, and the communications you have—will be private.

Personal Web-Based Email

Although most companies have policies that address use of the company's email system (see Chapter 3), many companies have no policy regarding employees accessing their personal email accounts from work using the company's equipment. At first blush, it might seem like overkill to limit an employee's ability to check a personal email account from work. After all, if the company doesn't want employees to send a lot of personal messages on its own system, shouldn't it allow them to access their own accounts, at least during breaks and lunch?

Unfortunately, it's not that simple. Personal email accounts, such as those available from Hotmail, Yahoo!, Comcast, and Gmail, are Web-based. When an employee accesses this type of account from work, messages sent and received bypass the employer's security system. This means bad things—such as viruses, Trojan horses, and spyware—can get in, and good things—like trade secrets—can get out, and the company will never know about it.

RELATED TOPIC

Is your workplace "BYOD"? This section addresses policy provisions for employee's use of their own personal email accounts, either when accessed using your company's equipment or when used to conduct business. Some companies have "bring your own device" (BYOD) policies, by which employees can use their own mobile devices—smartphones and tablets—to access the company's email, applications, and sometimes documents and files. This is different from the employee using a personal account (rather than a personal device) to conduct business, covered here. (For information on BYOD, see Chapter 9.)

Doing Business Via Personal Email

Even employees with the best intentions can create huge problems for a company via their personal email accounts. Take, for example, the common practice of employees sending work-related documents or messages to their personal email address. Most employees who do this are simply trying to make it easier to work from home; some are trying to get around an employer system that allows them to save only a limited number of messages by keeping those messages in their personal account. And still other employees automatically forward messages they receive at work to their personal account, to make sure they can access their email while home or traveling for business. What harm could that cause?

Plenty, as it turns out. Those work documents and messages are stored not on the company's servers but on the Internet, where they could potentially be accessed by people outside the company. What if the employee's ISP scans messages to send targeted advertising to the user? What if someone hacks into the ISP's servers? What if the employee's laptop is stolen, with a saved password that allows the thief easy access to the employee's Web-based account? This is especially problematic if the forwarded information is something the employer has an obligation to keep private, such as medical records, customer information, or company trade secrets.

Beyond the potential theft or exposure of company records, allowing employees to transact company business via their personal email accounts creates another big problem for the company: Some of its business records are out of its control. The company might not even know about key negotiations, discussions, and deals that are carried out on personal email. It won't have those records if it needs to recreate contract talks, review an employee's personnel file, or respond to a subpoena. And, employees may save documents long after they would have been purged from the company's records, which means there could be a "smoking gun" out there that would otherwise have been destroyed.

All companies should adopt a policy prohibiting employees from using their personal email accounts to transact company business. This includes not only using those accounts for business correspondence, but also transmitting any messages or files that might contain confidential information.

CAUTION

Beware of shadow IT. What do cloud-based file-sharing or storage services, mobile apps, and Hillary Clinton's private email server have in common? They are (potentially) all forms of shadow or stealth IT: technology that has been pressed into service outside the official channels of the employer's IT department. (Using personal email accounts for work is an old-school example of shadow IT, one followed not only by Ms. Clinton, but by one-third of government employees and one-half of private sector employees who responded to a recent poll by Alfresco Software, as reported in *The Wall Street Journal*.) It's easy to see why companies dislike shadow IT. Often, these solutions lack the security and record-keeping functions companies need. So why does shadow IT exist? Usually, because employees want or need a tech solution that the company doesn't yet have or support.

Don't Use Personal Email Accounts for Work

Employees may not use their own personal email accounts to transact Company business. This includes storing work-related documents and email messages in your personal email account, sending work to your personal email account, engaging in work-related communications (with customers, clients, or coworkers, for example) using your personal email account, or "bouncing" messages from your Company email to your personal email when you are out of the office.

Although employees may find these practices convenient, they can create significant security problems, expose confidential Company

> **Don't Use Personal Email Accounts for Work, continued**
>
> information, and compromise the Company's record-keeping obligations. If you work offsite (for example, at home or on business travel), please contact the IT department to find out how to safely transmit and protect Company information.

Accessing Personal Email Accounts at Work

The risks discussed above give employers very good reasons to simply prohibit employees from using their Web-based email accounts at work. However, many companies are uncomfortable with a total ban. Surveys show that one-half to three-quarters of responding companies have no policies on access to Web-based email. Some are probably unaware of the potential problems; others may simply think a policy banning employee access to their own email accounts is too Draconian.

Your company will have to decide, based on its culture, level of trust in its employees, and values, whether to adopt a total ban. Even if your company decides not to prohibit all access to personal email, however, it should still have a policy putting some limits on the practice.

Alternative 1: Banning Access to Personal Email

> **No Access to Personal Email**
>
> Accessing your personal email account from work creates security risks for the Company's computer system and network. Therefore, employees may not use Company equipment to access their personal email accounts.

Alternative 2: Allowing Access to Personal Email

Rules for Accessing Personal Email

Accessing your personal email account from work creates security risks for the Company's computer system and network. To help control these risks, employees must follow these rules when using Company equipment to access their personal email:

- You may access your personal email account during nonwork hours only.

- Do not open any personal email messages from an unknown sender. Personal email is subject only to the security controls imposed by your provider, which may be less strict than the Company's. If a personal message contains a virus or other malware, it could infect the Company's network.

- Before you open any attachment, you must scan it for viruses using the Company's antivirus software.

- You may not transact Company business using your personal email account, nor may you transmit any Company documents using your personal email account.

Monitoring or Blocking Personal Email

If your company decides to ban employee access to their personal email accounts, you can use blocking software to prevent employees from accessing common email sites such as Hotmail, Yahoo!, and so on. If your company's monitoring system allows it to see employee messages in their personal email accounts (for example, because you use software that tracks everything the employee types or captures a screenshot of employee computers), you should let employees know.

Be warned, however, that you may not have a legal right to actually read messages sent to and from an employee's personal email account, even if those messages are sent using company equipment. A few courts have held that an employer may not read personal messages (and particularly not messages exchanged with an attorney) in an employee's personal email account. This is especially so if the employer accesses the messages using the employee's password, as captured by monitoring software. Before looking at email messages in an employee's personal account, consult with a lawyer.

The exact language you put in your policy will depend on the type of monitoring or blocking tools your company uses. Here are a couple of examples:

Optional Policy Language for Blocking Access to Personal Web-based Email Sites:

> The Company's security software blocks access to many Web-based email sites. The fact that you can access a Web-based email site does not mean that you are free to check personal email using the Company's equipment, however.

Optional Policy Language for Keylogger Software:

> The Company's monitoring software keeps track of everything you type on your computer. Therefore, although the Company allows employees to access their personal email accounts using Company equipment, employees should not expect any messages they send or view from work to be private.

Lessons From the Real World

Damages may be appropriate against employer who read employee's personal email messages.

While Bonnie Van Alstyne worked at Electronic Scriptorium, Limited (ESL), the president of ESL—Edward Leonard—accessed her personal email account and read her email. Van Alstyne used this personal account for business from time to time, but also had a company email account.

Van Alstyne didn't find out about Leonard's surreptitious reading until she had been fired and filed a lawsuit for sexual harassment and other employment claims against ESL. ESL then sued Van Alstyne for business-related torts and, in the course of discovery in that case, provided several email messages as evidence that had been copied from Van Alstyne's personal account. It later came out that Leonard had accessed Van Alstyne's account "at all hours of the day" and from a variety of locations, and ultimately produced copies of 258 email messages he had taken from that account.

Van Alstyne asked for damages for Leonard's actions. Leonard and ESL were ultimately ordered to pay compensatory damages, punitive damages, and attorneys' fees and costs. On appeal, the court knocked out the compensatory damages awards because Van Alstyne hadn't proved that she suffered actual damages—out-of-pocket losses caused by the violation. However, the court found that it was appropriate to award punitive damages and attorneys' fees even if Van Alstyne couldn't prove any actual damages.

Van Alstyne v. Electronic Scriptorium, Limited, 560 F.3d 199 (4th Cir. 2009).

> CAUTION
>
> **Don't forget the acknowledgment form.** If your company adopts the Internet policy covered in this chapter, make sure you require employees to sign an acknowledgment form. You'll find a sample acknowledgment form and instructions on this book's online companion page; see the appendix for more information.

Putting It All Together: Sample Internet Policy

Here's a sample Internet use policy adopted by an independent bookstore. The store's buyer uses the Internet frequently, while most employees need Internet access occasionally to answer customer questions, but don't spend much time online. The store doesn't have the time, money, or staff to actively monitor employee Internet use, nor has it invested in monitoring or blocking software. Because it also has limited IT capability, the store has decided to simply prohibit employees from accessing inappropriate sites, downloading or streaming improper materials, participating in outside business ventures, making personal posts, or accessing their personal email accounts from work.

Sample Using the Internet Policy

Personal Use of the Internet

Our network and Internet access are for official Company business. Employees may access the Internet for personal use only outside of work hours and only in accordance with the other terms of this policy. An employee who engages in excessive Internet use, even during nonwork hours, may be subject to discipline.

Prohibited Uses of the Internet

Employees may not, at any time, access the Internet using Company equipment for any of the following purposes:

- To view websites that offer pornography, gambling, or violent imagery, or are otherwise inappropriate in the workplace.

- To operate an outside business, online auction, or other sales site; solicit money for personal purposes; or otherwise act for personal financial gain or profit.

- To download or copy software, games, text, photos, or any other works in violation of copyright, trademark, or other laws.

- To stream, run, or download any non–Company-licensed software program without the express consent of the IT department.

- To stream, run, or download music, video, games, widgets, or any form of multimedia, from the Internet.

- To read, open, or download any file from the Internet without first screening that file for viruses using the Company's virus detection software.

If you believe that your job may require you to do something that would otherwise be forbidden by this policy, ask your manager how to proceed.

Sample Using the Internet Policy (continued)

No Personal Posts Using Company Equipment

Employees may not use the Company's equipment to transmit their personal opinions by, for example, posting a comment to a blog or contributing to an online forum. Even if you don't identify yourself as a Company employee, your use of Company equipment could cause your opinion to be mistaken for the Company's view.

Internet Use Is Not Private

We reserve the right to monitor employee use of the Internet at any time. You should not expect that your use of the Internet—including but not limited to the sites you visit, the amount of time you spend online, and the communications you have—will be private.

Don't Use Personal Email Accounts for Work

Employees may not use their own personal email accounts to transact Company business. This includes storing work-related documents and email messages in your personal email account, sending work to your personal email account, engaging in work-related communications (with customers, clients, or coworkers, for example) using your personal email account, or "bouncing" messages from your Company email to your personal email when you are out of the office.

Although employees may find these practices convenient, they can create significant security problems, expose confidential Company information, and compromise the Company's record-keeping obligations. If you work offsite (for example, at home or on business travel), please contact the IT department to find out how to safely transmit and protect Company information.

No Access to Personal Email

Accessing your personal email account from work creates security risks for the Company's computer system and network. Therefore, employees may not use Company equipment to access their personal email accounts.

Instant Messaging

In This Chapter:

Policy Provisions for Instant Messaging

- ☐ Alternative 1: No Instant Messaging
- ☐ Alternative 2: No Use of Consumer Instant Messaging
- ☐ Alternative 3: Using Consumer Instant Messaging Software
- ☐ IM Usernames and Passwords
- ☐ Personal Use of IM
- ☐ IM Is Not Private
- ☐ All Conduct Rules Apply to IM
- ☐ IM Security
- ☐ Retaining and Deleting Instant Messages

nstant messaging ("IM") is a form of text-based real-time communication. Users operate a software program (referred to as a "client"), which allows them to see who else in their IM network (often called a "buddy list" or "contact list") is online. The user can initiate a conversation with an online contact by sending a message, which triggers a pop-up window on the contact's computer. If the contact responds, a running dialog unfolds on the screen until the conversation ends. All instant messages travel though a server operated by the IM company—for example, when you use America Online Instant Messenger (AIM), all of your text passes through AOL's servers.

Should you allow employees to use IM? If so, will you allow them to use commercial IM software or require them to use an enterprise IM (EIM) system licensed by the company, one designed for business use that incorporates legal and security concerns? What limits—on personal use and content, for example—will you place on employee use of IM? And how will you make sure that important messages transmitted via IM will be saved and available when the company needs them? This chapter explains your company's policy options.

To IM or Not to IM?

IM is a great medium for quick, vital exchanges, such as "contract signed," "shipment didn't arrive this a.m., when can we expect?" or "original order sold out; are 1,000 additional units available?" For that reason, certain businesses that rely on speed—stock trading and sales are two obvious examples—quickly adopted IM systems in order to connect the right people, right away.

There are other potential IM benefits for businesses, as well. For example, business users of IM can see who's logged in and immediately direct important questions or concerns to an appropriate person who can handle them quickly. In addition, employees who work offsite can use IM to interact more directly with coworkers than they could by phone or email. IM allows employees to multitask: IM software is intended to run in the background, so employees can do other work while still receiving and responding to important instant messages. IM also helps many companies perform more efficiently by eliminating telephone tag, email bounce messages, and even some of the need for business travel. And, enterprise products that integrate IM with other apps and functions, such as Slack, can greatly enhance team collaboration and communication.

IM May Increase Productivity

IM can be a distraction for employees. The message notification feature—which shows up on top of everything else on your screen—can be disruptive, and the fact that others know you are online can invite conversations for which you really don't have time. So, you may be surprised to learn that employees who use IM report fewer workplace interruptions than those who don't.

Almost 30% of those who responded used IM at work; interestingly, employees between the ages of 46 and 55 were most likely to do so. IM users were less likely to agree with the statement, "I rarely complete a work task without being interrupted," than nonusers. The survey also found that using IM doesn't increase an employee's overall communication time. In other words, IM replaces other forms of communication rather than adding to them.

R. Kelly Garrett and James N. Danziger, "IM=Interruption Management? Instant Messaging and Disruption in the Workplace," *Journal of Computer-Mediated Communication* 13(1) (2007).

As is true of the other technological innovations covered in this book, however, these advantages don't come without some concerns. Among them are:

- **Security risks.** IM systems can carry files, and hackers have learned how to exploit this feature—particularly on commercial IM systems—to infect users' machines. Once one machine is infected, the malware is usually programmed to propagate by transmitting itself to everyone on the user's contact list. Unlike typical contagions by email which take a day or two, IM virus infections spread in hours.

- **Loss of proprietary information.** As with all forms of communication, IM enables employees to quickly pass your company's proprietary information to third parties. In addition, unless you have a purely internal EIM system, all IMs travel via public third-party servers.

- **Messaging spam (spim).** Just in case your business is not getting enough unsolicited commercial messages, IMs can bring you more of the same, except now it's *instant.*

- **Archiving.** Although some EIMs come with built-in archiving, many consumer IM systems do not automatically archive exchanges (as is done with email). As a result, your company may not be able to produce requested IM documents in a lawsuit.

- **Loss of productivity.** Anyone who has used IM knows it can be a tremendous time sink. And unfortunately, because of the way IM works, it can be hard for the well-mannered to ignore that little pop-up window saying "how RU?" Most of us feel we have to respond at the risk of being rude.

- **Informality.** Something about the format of IM—and the fact that it was developed for use in chat rooms—makes users feel that it's strictly for informal social conversation. This can lead to a lack of professionalism in business-related IM, and to inappropriate jokes, comments, or gossip.

Beyond Informality ... the Saga of Maf54

In one of the most shocking tales of workplace misuse of IM, Mark Foley, the former Republican Congressman from Florida, resigned in 2006 after his sexual communications with former male pages—several of whom had saved the heated IM dialogs—became public.

Foley, identified as "Maf54," called one of the correspondents his "favorite young stud," told the former page he was picturing his "great legs" and "cute butt," and soon was into unprintable territory. (At the same time that these conversations were going on, Foley was also the Chairman of the House Caucus on Missing and Exploited Children, which introduced legislation targeting sexual predators.) Foley initially claimed that the messages he sent were innocuous and accused his opponent of dirty politics. Once several news sources printed excerpts from the saved IMs, Foley apologized and immediately resigned.

Alternative 1: Prohibiting IM

The initial decision your company must make is whether IM—either a commercial or enterprise system—has any place in your business. As you consider your company's options, remember that your employees may already use IM on their work computers. As a practical matter, this means that banning or placing strict limits on IM amounts to taking away something employees already have, which is much more difficult than preventing them from using it in the first place.

If you wish to halt current use (and future uses), your company must block downloads of consumer IM software and routinely audit employee computers to make sure they aren't breaking the rules. Banning IM may also limit your company's options in communicating with future clients, customers, suppliers, and business partners.

If your company nonetheless decides to ban IM altogether—perhaps your employees don't need to converse in real time, you have no or very few employees who work remotely, and your customers and clients don't expect your employees to be available via IM—you can use the policy language below. (You can also skip the rest of this chapter, which applies only to companies that have decided to allow IM in some form.)

Alternative 1: Prohibiting IM

> **No Instant Messaging**
>
> Because of the security risks associated with publicly available IM software, instant messaging is prohibited at our Company. Employees may not download or use personal IM software from the Internet to send or receive instant messages. For example, employees may not use Yahoo! Messenger, Windows Live Messenger, or Google Hangouts. Violation of this policy will result in discipline, up to and including termination.

Permitting IM

If your company decides against an outright IM ban, it has two primary options: It can allow IM only through its own enterprise software or it can allow employees to use consumer IM software.

Alternative 2: Allowing IM Via Enterprise Software

Using enterprise IM software allows your company to avoid some of the problems associated with publicly available IM systems. Your company controls the system, so it can monitor content, check for viruses and other malware, and control abuse. A company-wide IM system can also automatically save and store IM dialogs. And, because all employees will be on the same IM system, you won't face any compatibility problems. On the other hand, enterprise software generally lacks some of the flexibility associated with consumer IM. In particular, employees can communicate only with each other, not the outside world.

Still, an enterprise IM system is ideal for intracompany communications. If your company goes this route, it may also want to prohibit employees from using consumer IM systems. After all, most of the benefits of using a company system will be lost if you leave the back door open.

No Use of Consumer Instant Messaging Systems

To facilitate communication among employees, our Company has an internal instant messaging (IM) system.

Because of the security risks associated with publicly available IM software, employees may not download or use personal IM software from the Internet to send or receive instant messages. For example, employees may not use Yahoo! Messenger, Windows Live Messenger, or Google Talk. Violation of this policy will result in discipline, up to and including termination.

Alternative 3: Allowing IM Via Consumer IM Software

For some companies, especially those with significant numbers of tech-savvy employees, a common solution is to allow employees to (continue to) use consumer IM software and manage the attendant risks using gateway software: software that allows your company to monitor incoming and outgoing IM, scan messages for content and viruses, and archive IM conversations. If you choose this option, you should require employees to utilize your IT department for installation and maintenance of consumer IM systems.

> **Using Consumer Instant Messaging Software**
>
> Our Company makes instant messaging (IM) capability available to our employees. If you wish to use IM, you must notify the IT department and let them know which publicly available IM software you would like to use. The IT department will download the appropriate software and set up your IM account.
>
> Employees may not download or use any IM software on their own, without going through the IT department. Violation of this policy will result in discipline, up to and including termination.

Usernames

There's a reason most people sending IMs aren't using the names listed on their birth certificates: Their screen names allow them to operate behind a pseudonym, to make a statement or to just illustrate a sense of humor.

This is all well and good behind the closed doors of home, but your company really doesn't want its clients receiving business-related IM from babealicious10. If you allow employees to use IM, you'll need to make sure they adopt professional, straightforward usernames.

> **IM Usernames and Passwords**
>
> Employees will be assigned an IM user ID and password by the IT department. Employees may not change their user ID without permission.
>
> If you have a personal account with any IM software provider, you may not use Company equipment to access your personal account. You may use only the ID and password provided by the Company.

Personal Use of IM

Will your company limit IM to business use only, or will you permit personal use as well? Banning all personal use of IM has its risks, chief among them that your company will inconsistently enforce that ban. Employees who are disciplined for instant messaging conduct (while others get away with it) may claim that your company engaged in retaliation, discrimination, or unfair labor practices. (See Chapter 3 for more information on the dangers of adopting a rule that isn't consistently enforced.) The better practice, as is true of email, is to allow some personal use of IM. The sample policy language below echoes the personal use policy for email from Chapter 3.

Personal Use of IM

The IM system is intended for official Company business. Although you may send occasional personal instant messages, you may do so during nonwork hours only.

Privacy and IM Monitoring

Like your email policy, your IM policy must inform employees that their instant messages are not private, and it must reserve the company's right to monitor and read IMs at any time. Even if your company doesn't currently read employee IM, it may one day have to do so if an employee is accused of sending sexually harassing messages, transmitting trade secrets to a competitor, or using IM to spread false rumors about another employee, for example.

Lessons From the Real World

Instant messages on employee's work computer lead to search of home computer.

Brian Toon was the vice president of technology solutions at Quotient Inc. until October 31, 2005. In December 2005, Quotient sued Toon for breach of contract and interference with contractual relations, among other things. Quotient claimed that Toon allowed a former Quotient employee access to Quotient's computer system, trade secrets, and other proprietary information, so the former employee could compete against Quotient.

Almost immediately after filing the lawsuit, Quotient asked the judge to allow it to copy the contents of Toon's home computer. Quotient argued that it had discovered evidence on Toon's work computer, including instant messages in which Toon and the former employee discussed competing against Quotient. Quotient also claimed that it had discovered emails and IMs indicating that Toon was using his personal email account and home computer for similar discussions. Quotient asked the court to allow an expert to copy the contents of Toon's home computer, to make sure that no evidence was inadvertently destroyed or overwritten before the court could decide whether Toon would have to hand it over.

Toon opposed the motion, claiming that copying his home computer would invade his and his wife's privacy. Despite this argument, the court allowed his computer to be copied but not reviewed. If the court later determined that Quotient was entitled to view any of the contents, they could be reviewed by Toon's lawyer, so any private, privileged, or otherwise unrelated material could be withheld.

Quotient Inc v. Toon, Case No. 13-C-05-64087 (Md. Cir. Ct. 2005).

As discussed in Chapter 3, the key to successfully defending against an employee's invasion of privacy claim is to tell employees explicitly that their messages are not private. This is especially important in the context of IM, which seems so ephemeral. (Once the dialog box disappears from the screen, many employees mistakenly assume that it's gone forever and, therefore, can't be retrieved or read by their employer.) Knowing that IM will be read also provides a powerful deterrent to inappropriate content.

What your policy should say about monitoring depends on how your monitoring software works. If, for example, your company uses "keylogger" software that tracks everything an employee types, you should put that information in your policy. If your company uses gateway software that scans outgoing IM for questionable content, you should add that to your policy. You can find sample monitoring policy language in Chapter 3.

RELATED TOPIC

Deciding whether to regularly monitor employee communications can be a very tough call. This is especially true for companies that have positioned themselves, internally or externally, as creative, pro-employee, or simply as a "fun" place to work. (For information on the pros and cons of monitoring, see Chapter 3.)

IM Is Not Private

Instant messages sent and received on Company equipment are the property of the Company. We reserve the right to access, monitor, read, and/or copy instant messages at any time, for any reason. You should not expect that IMs you send using Company equipment—including messages that you consider to be, or label as, personal—will be private.

Lessons From the Real World

Employee's IM might be private if employer said it wouldn't read the messages.

Jeff Quon was a sergeant on the SWAT team of Ontario, California. He received a pager with wireless text-messaging capability for work, and was told that the department's email policy applied to use of the pagers. That policy said that personal use was a significant policy violation; that the city had the right to monitor all activity; that users should not expect privacy; and that obscene or suggestive messages were prohibited.

However, there was also an informal policy that applied to the pagers. The lieutenant in charge of administering employee use of the pagers told employees that each pager was allotted 25,000 characters per month, and that he would not audit their pagers as long as they paid any overage charges each month. The department did not audit anyone's pager messages for the first eight months after the pagers were issued.

Quon exceeded the character limit three or four times, and paid the overage each time. When Quon and another officer again went over the limit, the chief decided that the messages sent and received on certain pagers (including Quon's) should be audited to figure out whether the city should increase the number of allowed characters and whether the officers were using the pagers for personal reasons. Because the city could not access the messages themselves, it asked its carrier (Arch Wireless) to provide transcripts. Those transcripts revealed that many of Quon's messages were personal and some were sexually explicit. Quon, his wife, and two other people with whom he exchanged text messages sued for violation of their rights to privacy.

The 9th Circuit Court of Appeals found in Quon's favor, ruling that the city had violated his reasonable expectation of privacy. The U.S. Supreme Court did not agree, however. The Supreme Court found that, even if Quon had a reasonable expectation of privacy, the decision to

Lessons From the Real World, continued

read his text messages was justified. In the Supreme Court's view, that decision had a legitimate, work-related goal—to determine whether the city needed to change the character limit on its pagers—and was not excessive in scope, in that the city audited only two months' worth of messages and did not read any messages that had been sent outside of work hours.

Quon v. Arch Wireless Operating Co., 560 U.S. 746 (2010).

Inappropriate Content Rules

As email and IM have become more popular, they have also become vehicles for inappropriate conduct. The potential content problems your company might encounter in IM are essentially the same as it might find in email: harassment, inappropriate jokes, and so on. In fact, the extremely informal nature of IM makes it even more vulnerable to these types of problems.

If your company has adopted IM in some form, then you should make clear that your company's conduct rules apply with full force to IM.

All Conduct Rules Apply to IM

All of our policies and rules of conduct apply to employee use of instant messaging (IM). This means, for example, that you may not use IM to send harassing or discriminatory messages, including messages with explicit sexual content or pornographic images; to send threatening messages; or to reveal Company trade secrets.

Lessons From the Real World

Employee fired for IM message claims that he was reporting harassment.

Todd Bernier was fired from his job as an equities analyst at Morningstar, Inc., for sending an instant message to a coworker, Christopher Davis. Bernier felt that Davis, who is gay, had sexually harassed him by staring at his private parts while both were using the urinal. (During the litigation, it came out that Davis has a "lazy eye" that sometimes makes it appear that he's looking at something else while conversing.) Rather than using the company's harassment complaint process, Bernier sent an anonymous IM to Davis through the company's internal system, saying "Stop staring! The guys on the floor don't like it."

Unlike Bernier, Davis did use the company's complaint process, to claim that he had been sexually harassed. The company investigated. When questioned, Bernier denied sending the IM; he was fired several hours later. At the termination meeting, Bernier admitted sending the IM and explained why he did so. Bernier later sued Morningstar for sexual harassment and retaliation.

Bernier lost on both claims. The court found no evidence that the company knew he was claiming harassment. He didn't use the company's complaint process, sent the IM anonymously to a coworker, and then denied sending it. Even after Davis brought the IM to the company's attention, there was no reason for the company to infer that the sender of the IM—as opposed to the recipient—felt sexually harassed.

Bernier v. Morningstar, Inc., 495 F.3d 369 (7th Cir. 2007).

Viruses and Security Threats

IM can be especially vulnerable to viruses, worms, and bots because of the way these threats travel. Unlike spam, which often has a nonsensical subject line and is sent from an unknown source, IM malware looks like an actual message from someone known to the recipient. Once an IM security threat infects one person's account, it typically sends itself to everyone on that person's buddy list within hours. A buddy who opens the message or downloads an attached file then becomes the next infectious agent. If you have permitted IM in your company, you should adopt the policy below.

IM Security

To avoid viruses and other threats, employees should not open instant messages or file attachments from people and businesses they don't recognize. Even if you know the sender, do not open an IM attachment that has a strange name or is not referenced in the body of the IM. It may have been transmitted automatically, without the sender's knowledge.

If you believe your computer has been infected by a virus, worm, or other security threat to the Company's system, you must inform the IT department immediately.

Employees may not share their IM password with anyone, nor may they use another employee's IM account.

Retention and Deletion

Like email messages, instant messages are electronic records. This means not only that your company may have a need, or an obligation, to retain some of these records, but also that these documents may be subject to discovery in a lawsuit. IMs are probably less likely to contain important information that your company needs to keep, simply because instant messaging doesn't lend itself to formal correspondence (for example, job applications, contract negotiations, or performance feedback). Most IMs your company generates can safely be deleted once the conversation ends.

For those few IMs that may have to be retained, your policy should explain how employees can save them. (And, at the same time, your company should institute training procedures so that employees understand how to retain and archive such messages.) It should also explain that other IMs—those that the company isn't obligated to keep—should be deleted once they are dealt with.

Retaining and Deleting Instant Messages

Because instant messages are electronic records, certain IMs must be retained for compliance purposes. Please refer to our record-keeping policy for guidance on which records must be kept, and for how long. If you have any questions about whether and how to retain a particular IM, please ask your manager.

We discourage employees from storing instant messages that are not subject to the retention rules explained above. Please make a regular practice of deleting IMs once you have read and/or responded to them. If you need to save a particular message, you may print out a paper copy, archive the message, or save it on your hard drive or disk. The Company will purge IMs that have not been archived after _____ days.

CAUTION

Don't forget the acknowledgment form. If your company adopts the instant messaging policy covered in this chapter, make sure you require employees to sign an acknowledgment form. You'll find a sample acknowledgment form and instructions in at this book's online companion page; see the appendix for more information.

Putting It All Together: A Sample Instant Messaging Policy

Here's a sample IM policy adopted by a company with a large sales force. The company decides to allow use of consumer IM to facilitate communication between salespeople and their customers. Salespeople are paid on commission, so the company isn't too worried about them wasting time on personal IM. As a result, it has decided not to monitor IM, but only to reserve its right to do so.

Sample Instant Messaging Policy

Using Consumer Instant Messaging Software

Our Company makes instant messaging (IM) capability available to our employees. If you wish to use IM, you must notify the IT department and let them know which publicly available IM software you would like to use. The IT department will download the appropriate software and set up your IM account.

Employees may not download or use any IM software on their own, without going through the IT department. Violation of this policy will result in discipline, up to and including termination.

IM Usernames and Passwords

Employees will be assigned an IM user ID and password by the IT department. Employees may not change their user ID without permission.

If you have a personal account with any IM software provider, you may not use Company equipment to access your personal account. You may use only the ID and password provided by the Company.

Personal Use of IM

The IM system is intended for official Company business. Although you may send occasional personal instant messages, you may do so during nonwork hours only.

IM Is Not Private

Instant messages sent and received on Company equipment are the property of the Company. We reserve the right to access, monitor, read, and/or copy instant messages at any time, for any reason. You should not expect that IM you send using Company equipment—including messages that you consider to be, or label as, personal—will be private.

Sample Instant Messaging Policy (Continued)

All Conduct Rules Apply to IM

All of our policies and rules of conduct apply to employee use of instant messaging (IM). This means, for example, that you may not use IM to send harassing or discriminatory messages, including messages with explicit sexual content or pornographic images; to send threatening messages; or to reveal Company trade secrets.

IM Security

To avoid viruses and other threats, employees should not open instant messages or file attachments from people and businesses they don't recognize. Even if you know the sender, do not open an IM attachment that has a strange name or is not referenced in the body of the IM. It may have been transmitted automatically, without the sender's knowledge.

If you believe your computer has been infected by a virus, worm, or other security threat to the Company's system, you must inform the IT department immediately.

Employees may not share their IM password with anyone, nor may they use another employee's IM account.

Retaining and Deleting Instant Messages

Because instant messages are electronic records, certain IMs must be retained for compliance purposes. Please refer to our record-keeping policy for guidance on which records must be kept, and for how long. If you have any questions about whether and how to retain a particular IM, please ask your manager.

We discourage employees from storing instant messages that are not subject to the retention rules explained above. Please make a regular practice of deleting IMs once you have read and/or responded to them. If you need to save a particular message, you may print out a paper copy, archive the message, or save it on your hard drive or disk. The Company will purge IMs that have not been archived after 90 days.

Social Media, Blogs, and Beyond: Personal Posting on the Internet

In This Chapter:

Policy Provisions for Blogs and Personal Postings

☐ Personal Blogs and Online Posts

☐ No Posting Using Company Resources

☐ Guidelines for Online Postings

☐ Promoting the Company or Its Products or Services

Chances are very good that many of your company's employees are posting personal content on the Internet. They may be posting at their own blog or website, or they may be posting at social networking or community sites—for example, uploading photos to Instagram, adding comments to other websites, sending out tweets, exchanging parenting advice on a listserv, or swapping recipes in a chat room. In some cases, however, employees may use these avenues for personal expression to vent about coworkers, supervisors, customers, and other workplace issues. And, some may express personal opinions—unrelated to their job—that could harm the company's reputation.

Employers face a dilemma. Most are understandably wary about trying to "crack down" on personal postings. After all, social media pages, blogs, and other personal sites are often a creative outlet, a way for friends and people with similar interests to stay in touch, a place to share opinions and be part of a larger community of Xena fans, pug owners, single parents, or recycling enthusiasts. They are, in a word, personal, and few employers really want to snoop through their employees' personal writings or be known as the company that stifles personal expression.

Unfortunately, however, not all employees like their jobs. An employee blog or Facebook page that reveals company trade secrets, slams a company product that's about to be released, or threatens or harasses other employees can also be an unmitigated disaster for the company. Even posts that have nothing to do with work can create major workplace problems, if they express extreme and unpopular views, racist comments, or violent fantasies, for example. This chapter explains what you can and can't do in regulating employee posts, and provides policy language that gives employees some ground rules for Internet content. (For information and policy language on employee posts to company sites or pages, see Chapter 7.)

CAUTION

Rules for employee posts—especially on social media sites— are in flux. In recent years, the National Labor Relations Board (NLRB), the government agency that regulates labor and union issues, has come down hard on employers with social media policies that might restrict discussion of working conditions. Policy language that many companies have used for years has been struck down as too likely to lead employees to believe that they may not criticize the company's policies and practices online, in violation of the right employees have to freely discuss working conditions with each other. The legal terrain is changing rapidly in this area, so check your social media policy with a lawyer to make sure it complies with the most recent legal decisions.

Restrictions on Personal Posting

As an employer, you have the right to control what employees do with the time and equipment you pay for, generally speaking. When employees use their own computers and devices to express their own opinions on their own time, however, an employer's legal rights are more limited. An employer's practical ability to crack down on employee posting is also more restricted, not to mention an employer's incentive to take action that will undoubtedly alienate large numbers of employees.

In this situation, the best offense is a good defense. Your company can manage the potential legal exposure and bad publicity that could result from employee posts that cross the line—without going overboard in policing employee expression—by adopting a policy that lets employees know where the line is. This section explains some legal rules and practical considerations to keep in mind as you review your options.

CAUTION

If access to an employee site is restricted, don't go there. If an employee restricts access to a blog or website, an employer who breaks into the site can get into trouble. That's what happened when the vice president of Hawaiian Airlines used an employee's name and password to access a private website created by a Hawaiian pilot, where the pilot and other authorized visitors posted bulletins critical of the airline, its officers, and the pilots' union. The 9th Circuit Court of Appeals allowed the site's owner to go forward with his lawsuit against Hawaiian for violating the Stored Communications Act. (*Konop v. Hawaiian Airlines*, 302 F.3d 868 (9th Cir. 2002).) A federal district court in New Jersey reached the same conclusion in upholding a jury award for employees who were fired after a manager accessed an invitation-only Myspace page where employees vented about the company; the manager allegedly pressured an employee to give up her user name and password to access the site. (*Pietrylo v. Hillstone Restaurant Group*, 2009 WL 3128420 (D. N.J. 2009).)

How Do Company Policies Affect Employee Use of Social Media?

According to the "Social Media and the Workplace" report released in 2016 by the Pew Research Center, employees who use social media at work do so for both personal and work-related reasons. One-third of the employees who responded to the survey said they used social media at work to take a "mental break" from their jobs, and one-quarter said they did so to catch up with family and friends. On the other hand, one-quarter of those surveyed said they used social media to support professional connections, and significant percentages of employees said they also used social media to help solve work problems or to ask work-related questions.

Half of the employees surveyed said their employers had policies on employee use of social media. Although these policies tended to reduce the number of employees who reported using social media to take a break from their jobs or connect with family and friends, these policies also tended to reduce the number of employees who reported using social media to get information that helps them do their jobs.

Legal Protections for Employees Who Post Online

Not surprisingly, there are a host of laws that protect an employee's right to speak freely online. Here's a rundown:

- **Off-duty conduct laws.** A number of states have passed laws that prohibit employers from disciplining or firing employees for activities they pursue off-site, on their own time. Although some of these laws were originally intended to protect smokers from discrimination—they tend to include language protecting employees who "use legal products" while off duty—others protect any employee conduct that doesn't break the law. These laws could provide legal protection for an employee who keeps a blog or posts online while off the clock.

- **Protections for political views.** A handful of states protect employees from discrimination based on their political views or affiliation. In these states, disciplining an employee for personal posts that endorse a particular candidate or cause could be illegal.

- **Protections for "whistlebloggers."** An employee who raises concerns about safety hazards or illegal activity at work may be protected as a whistleblower (or a "whistleblogger," if the concerns are raised in a blog). Whistleblower protections recognize that the public good is served by employees who are willing to come forward with these types of complaints, and that very few employees will do so if they can be fired for it.

- **Prohibitions on retaliation.** A variety of employment laws protect employees from retaliation for claiming that their rights have been violated. If an employee's blog post complains of workplace discrimination, harassment, violation of the Family and Medical Leave Act, wage and hour violations, or other legal transgressions, that employee may be protected from disciplinary action.

 TIP

The First Amendment doesn't apply in private employment. Many employees mistakenly believe that the right to free speech and freedom of the press, enshrined in the First Amendment of the U.S. Constitution, protects their right to say or write whatever they want online, in a blog or otherwise. However, the Constitution only protects individual rights from government intrusion, not from the actions of private companies. If a state government tried to ban what private citizens could say on their blogs, that would raise a First Amendment issue. If the government isn't involved, however, the First Amendment doesn't come into play.

These days, the most active enforcer of employee rights online is the National Labor Relations Board (NLRB), the government agency that investigates and enforces the nation's labor and union laws. What do employee posts have to do with labor relations? Plenty, if employees are fired or disciplined for (or prohibited by policy from) communicating with each other about the terms and conditions of employment and joining together to bring their concerns to their employer. Employees enjoy these rights to communicate with each other and raise group concerns to their employer (called "protected concerted activity" or simply "Section 7 activity," after the provision of the National Labor Relations Act that creates them) whether or not they are represented by a union. In other words, all employers, whether unionized or not, must follow these rules.

In the last five years or so, the NLRB has shown great interest in going after employers who fire or discipline employees for posting critical comments about the company on social media sites or blogs. (You can find several NLRB reports on these cases at its website, www.nlrb.gov.) For example:

- A collections agency was found to have illegally fired an employee for Facebook posts complaining about her transfer. The employee used expletives and said she was done with being a good employee; her coworkers who were Facebook friends posted comments expressing support, criticizing the employer, and suggesting a class action lawsuit. Because the employees were discussing taking action regarding the terms of their employment, the NLRB concluded that they were engaged in protected concerted activity.

- A former employee posted to her own Facebook page that her former employer had incorrectly handled its tax paperwork, resulting in her owing money. Several current employees responded, including one who hit the "Like" button and another who claimed to owe money too and called the owner an expletive. The NLRB (and a federal Court of Appeals) found it illegal when the employer fired the employees.

- A server for a catering company posted an expletive-laden comment on his Facebook page, referring to a manager who had told employees to move more quickly. The post slammed the manager and the manager's family, and ended with "Vote YES for the UNION!" The NLRB found that the company's decision to fire the employee was illegal, despite the "distasteful" nature of the criticism, because it was part of an ongoing series of complaints and discussions about the way managers treated employees and the possibility of starting a union.

- A group of employees took to Facebook to complain about a coworker who they felt had been criticizing their performance. A conversation about the employer's policies toward its clientele ensued, then five of the employees were fired. The NLRB found the firings illegal, because the employees were discussing the terms of their employment and considering how to raise those concerns with their employer.

As part of these enforcement actions, the NLRB often finds that the employer's social media and posting policy is too broad, because it would tend to discourage employees from exercising their right to engage in Section 7 activity. The Board has objected to policies that prohibit disparagement or criticism of others; policies that require employees not to post "confidential" or "non-public" information (unless the policy illustrates the types of information covered, so as not to dissuade employees from discussing wages or other terms of employment); policies that require employees to avoid picking fights or discussing topics that are objectionable or inflammatory; and policies that require employees to check with a supervisor before posting.

Don't Ask Employees For Their Social Media Passwords

Many companies look online for publicly available information on job or promotion applicants, including on Facebook and other social networking sites. But the Maryland Department of Corrections took this common practice a step further when it asked employee Robert Collins to hand over his Facebook password during a job recertification interview.

The situation was publicized when the American Civil Liberties Union filed a lawsuit on Collins's behalf in 2011. Soon after, Maryland passed a law banning this practice, and Illinois followed suit. Now, about half the states have similar legislation; check the website of the National Conference of State Legislatures, www.ncsl.org, for up-to-date information.

Practical Concerns When Limiting Personal Posts

In addition to legal concerns, there are also practical reasons why your company should tread carefully when seeking to regulate personal blogs and online posts.

- **The "POS" factor.** Children on the Internet often use the acronym POS (for "parent over shoulder") to indicate that they can't speak freely because a parent has entered the room. Employees are very likely to see your company restrictions on personal posting at home in the same way: overly restrictive and unnecessarily intrusive. Why should an employer care whether employees post about their kitchen remodel, their children's health problems, or their favorite band? The more a company tries to limit what its employees do off duty, the more employees are likely to feel like prisoners or children, rather than valued members of a team.

- **Public relations concerns.** An employer that tries to prohibit or greatly restrict personal posting also runs into a potential public relations problem: The online community doesn't like—and will publicize—efforts to silence one of their ranks. The result could be a blog swarm or a Twit storm of bad PR for your company.

- **Enforcement problems.** It can be tough to enforce a restrictive policy on employee posts. If they post from home, how will you find out about it? Are you really going to dedicate human resources to finding and reading employee blogs and Facebook pages? If an employee uses a pseudonym and doesn't name your company or other employees, how are you going to know about the blog or page? How much time and effort is your company willing to put into policing employees' personal posts? For most companies, the answer is not much (if any).

Lessons From the Real World

Lockheed employee blows the whistle on YouTube.

Michael De Kort, an engineer at Lockheed Martin, was concerned about design flaws in work the company was doing to refurbish patrol boats for the Coast Guard. The flaws included blind spots in the boats' surveillance systems, security problems with the communications systems, and possible equipment malfunction in cold weather.

De Kort spoke to his supervisors, government investigators, and even members of Congress. He felt his concerns weren't being taken seriously, so he posted a video of himself talking about them on YouTube. Six months later, a government report confirmed some of his complaints. And, in January 2008, he received an award from the Society of Social Implications of Technology, for "high ethical standards in protecting or promoting the interests and safety of the public." Lockheed apparently didn't share the love for De Kort: He was fired shortly after posting the video, for what Lockheed said were cost-cutting reasons.

Adopting a Commonsense Policy

Online postings are easy to dash off and virtually impossible to erase completely once published. When employees aren't at work, they probably aren't thinking of the potential consequences of making fun of a coworker's accent or revealing little-known facts about a client. Most likely, they're simply trying to be funny and attract readers or "likes."

What can your company do to curb inappropriate employee posts without going overboard? Adopt a policy letting employees know that their personal blogs could get them in trouble at work, and explain what types of content could be problematic.

Having a written policy on personal posts puts employees on notice that their personal writings could get them into professional trouble (something that many employees seem not to fully understand). In short, it may remind them to think before they publish posts that cross the line.

To start your company's policy, you'll want to assure employees that the company supports their personal creative efforts, while also reminding them that they shouldn't violate the company's rights or the rights of customers and coworkers.

Personal Blogs and Online Posts

Our Company recognizes that some of our employees may choose to express themselves by posting personal information on the Internet through personal websites, social media, blogs, or chat rooms, by uploading content, or by making comments at other websites or blogs. We value our employees' creativity and honor your interest in engaging in these forms of personal expression on your own time, should you choose to do so.

However, problems can arise when a personal posting identifies or appears to be associated with our Company, or when a personal posting is used in ways that violate the Company's rights or the rights of other employees.

No Posting Using Company Resources

Your policy should prohibit employees from using the company's computer systems to write or publish personal posts.

Social Media Freedom More Important Than Salary to Generation Z

In 2011, Cisco surveyed more than 2,800 college students and young professionals in 14 countries—the so-called "millenials" or Generation Z. Given the generally crummy state of the economy at the time, it seemed logical that those who were looking for jobs (or soon to be) would list their primary concerns as, well, just whether they'd be able to find work, along with salary, salary, and salary.

But no. According to this survey, it's all about social networking, portable electronic devices, and working from home or other remote locations. Here are a few choice bits:

- More than half said that if their company banned access to social media sites from work, they would either turn down a job offer or find a way to get around the prohibition.
- 40% of college students—and 45% of young professionals—said they would accept lower paying work if it offered more flexibility regarding social media access, mobility, and device choice.
- About 70% said they should be allowed to access personal sites and social media sites using company-owned devices.

No Posting Using Company Resources

You may not use Company resources to create or maintain a personal blog, personal website, or personal page on a social networking site, or to upload content or make personal postings online, nor may you do so on Company time.

Ground Rules for Posting Content

Your company's policy should give employees some guidelines for posting online, whether to personal blogs, personal websites, social media, or community sites. Your goal here is to make sure employees know that they post at their own risk. Many employees don't realize that they can get into personal legal trouble for what they post. Despite a number of well-publicized firings based on employee posts, some employees still don't realize that writing about work can lead to the unemployment line.

Fired for Online Posting

With the growing legal protections for employees who post online, you may be surprised to learn that 18% of employers surveyed by Careerbuilder in 2015 said they had fired an employee for something posted on social media. You may feel less surprised when you learn some of the actual things employees say online that lead to their termination:

- Heather Armstrong was fired by her employer (whom she never identified on her blog) for humorous posts about annoying habits of her coworkers and company management, what she actually did when she was supposed to be working at home, and other things. Her website, www.dooce.com, brought the word "dooced" to the modern lexicon (it means to get fired for blogging).
- Two employees of Domino's pizza were fired after they posted a YouTube video in which one of them put cheese up his nose before putting it on a sandwich; they were also hit with felony charges.
- Matt Donegan, a reporter and editor, was fired by *The Dover Post* after his MySpace blog included an entry that complained about his African-American neighbors partying late into the night and speculated whether similar circumstances might have led to the assassination of Martin Luther King, Jr. Donegan said the post was intended as a joke. His employer was not LOL.

By making sure employees know the risks, and setting down some ground rules for posts that deal with your company, your policy can encourage employees to stop and think before they hit "publish." At the same time, your policy must not discourage employees from sharing concerns—and even complaints—about working conditions, pay, and so on with coworkers.

Guidelines for Online Posting

You are legally responsible for content you post to the Internet, in a blog, social media site, or otherwise. You can be held personally liable for defaming others, revealing trade secrets, and copyright infringement, among other things.

All of our Company policies apply to anything you write in a personal blog, post to the Internet, or upload to the Internet. This means, for example, that you may not use personal postings to harass or threaten other employees or reveal Company trade secrets or confidential information, such as internal reports or confidential company communications.

If, in the process of making a personal post or upload on the Internet, you identify yourself as an employee of our Company, whether by explicit statement or by implication, you must clearly state that the views expressed in your post, or at your blog, social media page, or website, are your own, and do not reflect the views of the Company.

You may not use the Company's trademarks, logos, copyrighted material, branding, or other intellectual property in a way that violates intellectual property law.

The Company may have a legal duty not to disclose certain facts, such as information on stock offerings. Employees must follow the law and refrain from making any prohibited disclosures.

Rules for Endorsements

Does your company sell its products on sites that allow users to comment or review the products, such as Amazon? Does your company appear on online review sites, such as Yelp? Are your company's products discussed in user boards, blogs, and/or social networking sites? If so, you need to make sure that employees always identify themselves—and their relationship to your company—if they post content or reviews of your company's products. In fact, it's a good idea to require employees to identify themselves in any post about the company to avoid the possibility of misleading readers.

Is That You, Rahodeb?

Whole Foods cofounder John Mackey posted more than 1,000 entries on Yahoo Finance's online bulletin board over seven years, under the name "Rahodeb" (a mashup of his wife's name, Deborah). He wrote a lot about Whole Foods, expressed some negative opinions about rival (and acquisition target) Wild Oats, and on occasion paid himself anonymous compliments, such as "I like Mackey's haircut. I think he looks cute!" Mackey finally revealed his true identity online, after losing a bet.

Andrew Martin, "Whole Foods Executive Used Alias," *The New York Times*, July 12, 2007.

The Federal Trade Commission (FTC), the federal government agency that regulates deceptive advertising and other consumer protection matters, has issued regulations governing endorsements and testimonials about products, including statements that appear online. The purpose of these rules is to make sure consumers fully understand the relationship between the person making the endorsement and the product, so they can make informed decisions about how much weight to give the endorser's statement. A statement by an actor or a paid spokesperson probably isn't as credible as a statement by an actual user of the product, for example. The FTC rules seek to make the relationship between the product and the person raving about it explicit.

What do these rules have to do with employee posts? If employees post anything about your company's products online, they must identify themselves as employees of the company. The FTC has said that an employment relationship is the type of connection that a consumer would want to know about in evaluating product endorsements. So, your policy must tell employees that if they post reviews or other types of statements about company products, they must be up front about their relationship to the company.

Promoting the Company or Its Products or Services

Do not engage in covert marketing or endorsements for the Company or its products or services. If you post anything about the Company, you must identify yourself as a Company employee. You are legally required to identify your employment relationship if it might be relevant to a consumer's decision to patronize our company or your failure to do so could be misleading to readers. This means, for example, that employees may not post anonymous online reviews of Company products or promotional statements about the Company in which they fail to identify themselves as employees. You must also identify yourself as an employee in your online post if you endorse or review Company products or services on social media. It is not enough to identify the Company as your employer in your profile page, for example.

Espresso Addict, Indeed: Company Employee Posts 12 Product Reviews

As reported on his own blog and *The Wall Street Journal* blog, Russ Taylor was shopping for an espresso machine. He was reading Amazon reviews of high-end coffee products when he noticed that someone named "T. Carpenter" had written 12 reviews, all giving five stars to products made by DeLonghi. In fact, he noticed that the ubiquitous reviewer had submitted one review that said "instead of buying two different machines for my family I bough[t] only this DeLonghi machine," yet had posted a separate review of a different espresso maker the same day.

Smelling a rat, Taylor did a Google search and found that someone named Tara Carpenter worked as a communications manager for DeLonghi. Taylor got in touch with DeLonghi, but received no substantive response. That changed when Taylor passed the news item on to *The Wall Street Journal*. DeLonghi took that phone call, and confirmed to the *Journal* that Carpenter worked for the company and posted the reviews. In its defense, DeLonghi pointed out that it saw no false statements in the reviews, and that its employees "are passionate about the products we make and sell." Indeed.

CAUTION

The FTC tells employers to remind employees about their endorsement policy. In 2015, the FTC updated its endorsement guidance by adding some questions and answers that specifically address social media. In that update, the agency indicated that employers don't have to review employees' social media posts to make sure they are in compliance, as long as the employer has a proper endorsement policy, reminds employees periodically of the policy (particularly if the employer encourages employees to review company products), and takes steps to correct any employee posts that don't follow the rules.

Friending at Work

Socializing among coworkers doesn't just take place during coffee breaks, lunch, and after-work happy hours anymore. Now, coworkers can also keep up with each other's romances, family outings, candid photos, and daily doings online, too, by "friending" each other on Facebook, following each other on Twitter, or otherwise joining each other's online social networks.

Unfortunately, what many see as good clean fun can quickly become a workplace problem. What if one coworker is left out of the network and feels excluded from the team? What if a manager posts photos of himself at a rally opposing gay marriage—and a gay subordinate starts to wonder if his sexual orientation is preventing him from getting promoted? What if a manager sends a friend request to a subordinate who really doesn't want to reciprocate, but feels she can't turn down her manager? Social media create many opportunities to blur the line between work lives and private lives, sometimes with unprofessional and unkind results.

Some companies prohibit managers from friending subordinates, period. There are legal reasons why such a restrictive policy makes sense, if the subordinate ever has a gripe with the supervisor or the company. In that situation, the subordinate (or his or her lawyer, in the worst case scenario) could sift through every post the manager has made, looking for evidence of discriminatory beliefs, inappropriate behavior, illegal or unprofessional goings on inside the company, and so on.

At the same time, however, a policy this restrictive will almost certainly meet with tremendous resistance. After all, it tells employees whom they may communicate with on their own time, using their own equipment. Also, this type of policy would be very difficult to enforce. While a cost-benefit analysis might convince some companies to adopt restrictions like these, most won't want to go this far in dictating employee behavior off the job.

The sensible middle ground here is to alert employees to the problem and ask them to use discretion when social networking with work colleagues.

> **Interacting Online With Colleagues**
>
> The Company does not tolerate conduct or communications toward work colleagues that violate company policy—such as sexual harassment, bullying, or threats—whether they take place online or off.

CAUTION

Don't forget the acknowledgment form. If your company adopts the personal blogs and online posting policy covered in this chapter, make sure you require employees to sign an acknowledgment form. You'll find a sample acknowledgment form and instructions at this book's online companion page; see the appendix for more information.

Putting It All Together: A Sample Blog and Personal Post Policy

Here's a sample blog and personal post policy adopted by a company that designs software. The company encourages employee creativity and independent thinking, so it doesn't want to be seen as banning employees' personal expression. Many of its employees keep their own blogs and post to a variety of online forums, however, so the company decides that it needs to establish guidelines.

Sample Personal Blogs and Online Posts Policy

Our Company recognizes that some of our employees may choose to express themselves by posting personal information on the Internet through personal websites, social media, blogs, or chat rooms, by uploading content, or by making comments at other websites or blogs. We value our employees' creativity and honor your interest in engaging in these forms of personal expression on your own time, should you choose to do so.

However, problems can arise when a personal posting identifies or appears to be associated with our Company, or when a personal posting is used in ways that violate the Company's rights or the rights of other employees.

No Posting Using Company Resources

You may not use Company resources to create or maintain a personal blog, personal website, or personal page on a social networking site, or to upload content or make personal postings online, nor may you do so on Company time.

Guidelines for Online Posting

You are legally responsible for content you post to the Internet, in a blog, social media site, or otherwise. You can be held personally liable for defaming others, revealing trade secrets, and copyright infringement, among other things.

All of our Company policies apply to anything you write in a personal blog, post to the Internet, or upload to the Internet. This means, for example, that you may not use personal postings to harass or threaten other employees or reveal Company trade secrets or confidential information, such as internal reports or confidential Company communications.

Sample Personal Blogs and Online Posts Policy (continued)

If, in the process of making a personal post or upload on the Internet, you identify yourself as an employee of our Company, whether by explicit statement or by implication, you must clearly state that the views expressed in your post, or at your blog, social media page, or website, are your own, and do not reflect the views of the Company.

You may not use the Company's trademarks, logos, copyrighted material, branding, or other intellectual property in a way that violates intellectual property law.

The Company may have a legal duty not to disclose certain facts, such as information on stock offerings. Employees must follow the law and refrain from making any prohibited disclosures.

Promoting the Company or Its Products or Services

Do not engage in covert marketing or endorsements for the Company or its products or services. If you post anything about the Company, you must identify yourself as a Company employee. You are legally required to identify your employment relationship if it might be relevant to a consumer's decision to patronize our company or your failure to do so could be misleading to readers. This means, for example, that employees may not post anonymous online reviews of Company products or promotional statements about the Company in which they fail to identify themselves as employees.

You must also identify yourself as an employee in your online post if you endorse or review Company products or services on social media. It is not enough to identify the Company as your employer in your profile page, for example.

Interacting Online With Colleagues

The Company does not tolerate conduct or communications toward work colleagues that violate company policies—such as sexual harassment, bullying, or threats—whether they take place online or off.

Company-Sponsored Social Media

In This Chapter:

Policy Provisions for Company-Sponsored Social Media

☐ Our Company's Social Media Presence

☐ Who May Post

☐ Guidelines for Employees Who Post

☐ Identify Yourself

☐ You Are Responsible for Your Posts

☐ Handling Comments

Does your company have a business blog, pages on social networking sites (like Facebook or LinkedIn), a Twitter feed, or a YouTube channel? If so, you're in good company. These days, it's the rare business that doesn't have some presence in social media. These tools offer great opportunities to market a company and its products, to reach consumers and potential employees, and to position the company as a player in the field. Visibility on the Web—particularly in the places where coveted customers socialize, research products, and shop—can translate directly into increased brand loyalty and higher revenues.

Sounds great, right? But it doesn't happen by itself. Somebody has to write all those posts, comments, and tweets for your company's social media pages. The people your company taps to handle these online communications must have some guidance on acceptable and unacceptable content. Otherwise, they could unknowingly fall into the traps for unwary bloggers and posters discussed in Chapter 6, from defamation and copyright claims to invasion of privacy, disclosure of trade secrets, and public relations disasters. Only this time, your company will share the liability—and suffer most of the harm—for inappropriate or illegal employee posts.

RELATED TOPIC

For policy language and information on employees' personal posts, see Chapter 6. This chapter covers the company's online content: the social media posts employees write for the company as part of their jobs. Personal posts—such as an employee's own Facebook page, YouTube videos, or blog feeds—are covered in Chapter 6.

The employees who handle your company's social media presence need clear guidelines. The success of social media is based on attracting the most viewers through immediate interaction. Because social media places a premium on fresh information (as well as the humorous, clever, and hip), there is often a temptation to resort to the lowest common denominators in order to achieve viral success. Employees may, for example, be tempted to cross the lines from edgy humor into bad taste; or to create a news scoop by leaking a company secret. This chapter provides policy language that will help your employees understand how to stay on the right side of the line when posting to your company's social media pages.

How the Fortune 500 Use Social Media

According to an annual survey conducted by the University of Massachusetts, the vast majority of the Fortune 500 uses social media. However, there have been big changes in recent years in the most popular methods and platforms:

- 21% of the companies have a blog, down from 31% in 2014 and 34% in 2013.
- Use of YouTube has also declined, from a high of 69% in 2013 to 64% in 2015.
- Company use of Facebook and Twitter has declined slightly in the past year, but about three-quarters of the companies use both.
- Flashes in the pan? Companies that used Foursquare and Pinterest spiked in 2014, then declined markedly for 2015.
- The most significant increases came in company use of Instagram, up from 20% in 2014 to 33% in 2015, and Glassdoor, making its first appearance in the survey in 2015 at a whopping 87%.
- LinkedIn is still the big winner, logging the most company users at 93%.

Why Post?

A lot of attempts at social media quickly peter out. Statistics show that many company blogs expire from lack of interest, corporate Facebook fan pages become inactive, and Twitter feeds dissolve into the vapors. One of the main reasons for these failures is that so many companies jumped on the Web 2.0 bandwagon because it was "the next big thing," without giving much thought to what they hoped to accomplish with their blog or social networking page. The result for many companies was a series of glorified public relations posts that did not provide any real value to customers and, therefore, didn't attract much of a following.

What makes social media unique is that it is an interactive, constantly changing medium: Unlike a regular website, which generally provides static information, social networking tools facilitate communication. The result may be a two-way conversation, as when a customer posts a comment on your company's Facebook page, then your company responds, directly or online. Or, it could be a much larger discussion. If a new regulation affects your industry, for example, your in-house expert might write about it on the company's blog, citing to other experts who have weighed in and news articles on the topic. Your blog may then be cited by other blogs and news articles in turn, creating an ongoing conversation that can be followed by anyone who's interested. This type of communication generates media hits for your company, boosts your search engine optimization (SEO), shows that you are up on important issues in your industry, and brings in more readers (some of whom will, hopefully, turn into customers).

Whatever your plans include, if you're asking employees to represent your company online and to be its written voice and public face, it's only fair to tell them what you want them to do in that capacity. In other words, you should start your policy only *after* you've given some thought to where your company wants to be online and what you want to accomplish there.

That will depend on many variables, including your field, your products or services, your customer base, your resources, and more. The introductory language provided below will work for many companies that want to use social media to market and publicize the company and its products.

> **Our Company's Social Media Presence**
>
> Social media tools, including Company-sponsored blogs and microblogs, social networking sites, video or picture sharing sites, wikis, and other means of communicating online, are an important part of our Company's face to the public. These social media offer opportunities to shape opinion about our products and our company, to communicate directly with customers and clients, to provide added value for our customers, and to be part of the online conversation about important developments in our field.

If your company has more specific goals in creating or maintaining a social media presence, you should include them at the end of this paragraph. Here are some examples:

> Our Company's affiliation with the athletes who use our products is at the heart of our marketing efforts. We hope to build customer interest in our company by featuring the achievements of our sponsored athletes—and offering opportunities for amateur athletes who use our products to join the conversation—in all of our social media efforts.

> We want to use social media to educate consumers and to generate interest in our soy-based line of meat replacement products, using content that will appeal to and expand our customer base. This might include things like recipes and information on the health benefits of soy products, vegetarian diets, organic foods, and so on.

Our social media strategy centers on our connection with the San Francisco Bay Area, where we have been based for more than a century. We want to provide social media content that emphasizes and builds this relationship, such as information about San Francisco history (and our role in it, including helping to rebuild after the 1906 earthquake!), other local businesses, facts and lore about the city, and features on local customers.

Who May Post

Your policy should specify that employees must be authorized to post content to company sites. Some companies—such as those in the fields of high-tech or information services—may decide to allow many employees to post. At other companies, only a select few will have the expertise and savvy to speak for the company. Either way, your policy should explain your method of authorizing employees to represent the company via social media.

Your company should also provide some training for employees who will post on the company's behalf. There are many posting pitfalls for the unwary and your company will likely be responsible for employee posts to official company sites, so it is absolutely vital to train employees who will represent the company online.

Who May Post

Only authorized employees may set up or post to Company-sponsored blogs or microblogs, social networking pages, or other social media. Authorization is granted by [*position responsible for designating employees who may post, such as "the Director of Online Marketing"*]. Before you begin posting content, you must attend social media training.

Who Owns That Twitter Handle?

Often, it's perfectly clear that a social media page, website, or Twitter feed is corporate. For example, if a company's website has a blog or Facebook page, and a number of employees post work-related items on the company's behalf, any particular employee would have a hard time arguing that he or she "owned" the account.

However, the situation might look different if a particular account is closely identified with a particular employee, especially if that employee takes steps to mingle the personal and professional. Here are a couple of examples:

- Noah Kravitz started a Twitter account while he was employed at PhoneDog. The account was under his name (PhoneDog_Noah), he linked it to his personal email account, and he posted items both personal and professional. When he left the company, he changed his handle to NoahKravitz and kept tweeting on the account. PhoneDog sued to stop him, arguing that his followers were a type of customer list, and therefore that Kravitz had misappropriated the company's trade secret.

- Linda Eagle, the founder of EdComm, opened a LinkedIn account in 2008. She used the account to promote the company and her own accomplishments, as well as to stay in touch with social and professional contacts; an EdComm employee had her account password and helped her maintain it. She left the company following a buyout, and EdComm changed her LinkedIn password and continued to use the account. Eagle sued for misappropriation of her account.

If you are bringing on employees with existing social media accounts that you'd like them to use for business, or if your employees mingle personal with business posts on an account that you believe belongs to your company, you can clarify ownership of the account through a written agreement. As this area of law is just beginning to develop, you should talk to a lawyer if you're facing this issue.

Guidelines for Posting

Your policy should provide some basic guidance for employees who post on company-sponsored sites and pages. After all, you don't want an employee to announce a deal on the company blog that hasn't yet been finalized, disclose marketing secrets related to an unreleased product, or use copyrighted images from a hot movie trailer without permission. At the same time, you want employees to post content that's interesting, relevant, and reflects positively on your company.

The sample policy language below includes some common guidelines for employee posts.

Guidelines for Employees Who Post

1. **Be respectful.** When you post about the Company, its products and employees, customers, and competitors, use good judgment. Make sure your posts are professional and respectful. It's fine to disagree, as long as you do so in a civil way and you're not offensive.

2. **Add value.** We expect you to write about new developments and trends in your area of expertise. Don't just recycle news or posts; add your perspective and provide useful advice to enable consumers to better use our products and services.

3. **Post often.** We want readers to return and see what's new at our Company, and the best way you can help make that happen is to post at least weekly.

4. **Be part of the conversation.** When appropriate, link to other sites, articles, blogs, and media on the same topic. And of course, link to our Company site when appropriate.

Guidelines for Employees Who Post, continued

5. **Accuracy counts.** Before you publish a blog post or a social media entry, review it for accuracy. When writing about Company business, check with the appropriate people in-house to make sure you've got the facts straight. If you later learn you've made a mistake, say so and correct it.

6. **Avoid inappropriate topics.** We want you to generate interest, but there are many ways to do that without offending readers or placing the Company in the midst of a controversy. All company policies, including those that prohibit harassment, discrimination, and un-professional conduct, apply with equal force to your online posts.

7. **Respect ownership of intellectual property.** Don't copy or use work by someone else (including text, photos, and video) without proper authorization and, if required, attribution. If you're referring to a copyrighted story, keep your quotes short; if you want to refer to another's work, it's best to link to it in its entirety.

8. **Keep the Company's secrets.** Don't refer to or reveal the Company's trade secrets and proprietary information. This includes stock offerings, financials, products in development, and other confidential information. If you aren't sure whether to reveal particular information in your post, speak to your manager.

9. **Maintain customer and employee privacy.** Do not mention customers by name or identifying details without authorization from your manager. If you want to discuss or mention coworkers in your posts, you must get their permission first.

10. **Ask—and think—before you post.** Remember, your posted content represents you and the Company to the public. All of us want that representation to be positive. If you aren't certain that what you plan to post is appropriate and legal, check with your manager before you post.

Defamation in 140 Characters or Less

Some people find it hard to express themselves or say anything meaningful within the 140-character limit set by Twitter. Others, apparently, can say enough to spark a lawsuit (or at least the threat of one). Here are a few examples of alleged defamation by Tweet:

- In what may be the first Twitter lawsuit, Courtney Love was served with legal papers after reportedly using her Twitter account to call fashion designer Dawn Simorangkir a prostitute, drug addict, and "nasty lying hosebag thief." (And those are only seven of the words ...).

- Amanda Bonnen tweeted her friend to say, "Who said sleeping in a moldy apartment is bad for you? Horizon realty thinks it's okay." Horizon, which owned the apartment building where she lived, was not amused: It sued her for libel and asked for $50,000 in damages. The irony: Before the lawsuit, Bonnen's Twitter feed (and the allegedly libelous comments) were seen only by Horizon and her reported 20 followers; once the lawsuit was filed and the story picked up by the *Chicago Sun-Times*, thousands more readers learned about Bonnen's "moldy apartment."

- Kim Kardashian got slapped with a lawsuit by Dr. Sanford Siegel, originator of "the cookie diet." According to published reports, Siegel's site linked to an article in which someone claimed that Kardashian was on the diet. Kardashian responded on Twitter, saying "Dr. Siegel's Cookie Diet is falsely promoting that I'm on this diet. NOT TRUE! I would never do this unhealthy diet. I do Quick Trim!" Siegel sued for libel over nine of those characters: the ones that spell "unhealthy."

Authorship and Disclaimers

In the recent past, the Internet allowed only one-way communication. A company developed a basic website that provided information and perhaps allowed customers to place orders, and that was it. No individual names were associated with the site: It represented the company as a whole.

With the advent of Web 2.0, however, the monologue has become a discussion. Social media allows many voices to speak and respond to each other—and readers want to know who those voices are. These new communication tools place a premium on point of view, perspective, and personality. That's why most companies that have a social media presence ask employees to identify themselves by name and title, as the policy language below does.

Identify Yourself

When you post any type of content to Company-sponsored social media, such as our Facebook or Twitter pages, you must identify yourself by name and by your position at the Company. Anonymous posting or posting under pseudonyms or aliases is prohibited. The same rule applies if you are posting comments on behalf of the Company to one of our competitors' social media accounts, websites, or product pages.

CAUTION

Employees must reveal their employment relationship when posting comments about your company or its products. The Federal Trade Commission, which interprets and enforces the laws prohibiting deceptive advertising, has issued regulatory guidelines on product endorsements, including those that appear in social media. The rules make clear that employees who discuss their company's products in online posts—for example, a comment to a blog or social networking page—must identify themselves as company employees, to avoid leading other readers to believe that they are just ordinary consumers who happen to LOVE what your company makes. (For more on these rules, see Chapter 6.)

Some companies also require employees to post a conspicuous disclaimer on their company blogs or comments to social media pages, stating that the posted content represents their own views, not necessarily the views of the company. From a legal perspective, it's not clear that a disclaimer like this carries much weight. If the employee is posting on company time and the company dime, chances are very good that the company will be vicariously liable for the employee's activities, particularly if the company's name appears on the masthead of the blog or page.

On the other hand, requiring employees to post a disclaimer has a couple of benefits. First of all, it reminds employees to take responsibility for what they post. Your company may well be liable for what employees post, but it won't be alone at the defense table: The employee could also be personally liable for posts that break the law or cause personal injury (such as defamation or harm to reputation). Second, it signals to customers (and your stockholders) that the company doesn't necessarily agree with every opinion an employee puts into the blogosphere, which may prove helpful if you need to distance yourself from a post for public relations reasons. Include the language below in your policy if you want employees to claim their opinions for themselves.

You Are Responsible for Your Posts

Remember, you are legally responsible for what you post online, whether on a personal site or a Company-sponsored site. You can be held personally liable for defaming others, revealing trade secrets, and copyright infringement, among other things. All Company policies apply to your online posts on Company-sponsored sites.

All employees who post content to Company sites and pages must include the following disclaimer:

"The posts on this page express my own views and opinion, and do not necessarily reflect the views of [_company name_]."

Employer Sued for Employee's Blog Posts: The Patent Troll Tracker Affair

Rick Frenkel, a lawyer who worked as the director of intellectual property at Cisco Systems, maintained a blog under the name "Patent Troll Tracker," in which he wrote about patent trolls: a derogatory term for someone who sues for patent infringement but who does not make or sell any products using the patented technology. The blog's author was anonymous until Frenkel revealed his name and affiliation with Cisco, following the posting of a $15,000 "bounty" for his identification.

Once Frenkel's identity was known, he, Cisco, and two of its executives were sued over blog posts that allegedly disparaged attorneys who filed a patent suit against Cisco. Frenkel's blog was anonymous; it was not an official company blog nor did it appear on the company's website. Nonetheless, Cisco eventually took responsibility for the blog posts and Frenkel was dropped from the lawsuit, which settled.

Handling Comments

One of the features that makes social media unique is the ability for readers to respond with comments. When your company has blogs, pages on networking sites such as Facebook, or a Twitter feed, third parties can join the conversation. And, that conversation is memorialized under your company's name. This can be enormously helpful in building community, word of mouth, and loyalty among your company's customers. But it can also mean pages littered with spam, unfounded criticisms, and outright ranting.

If your company doesn't yet have a blog, you will be amazed by the amount of spam you receive as comments, and by the percentage of actual comments that are so inappropriate as to be unprintable. One way to handle this is to simply turn off the comments feature. This serves the purpose of keeping unwanted content off your site, as well as saving you the time and resources of screening comments. However, it also defeats one of the goals of participating in social media in the first place: creating an interactive relationship. And, for social networking sites like a Facebook fan page, turning off comments altogether is difficult and removing selected comments is nearly impossible (without soliciting Facebook's help). People come to these sites to communicate and participate.

Another way to handle comments is to moderate them, allowing all comments that are legitimate (that is, they aren't spam or an advertising link to another site) and not offensive. (Or, as Intel's Social Media Guidelines put it, post "the Good, the Bad, but not the Ugly.") What you don't want to do is pick and choose among comments, posting only the most flattering and sending complaints or criticisms to the virtual garbage bin. You absolutely should screen for appropriateness (in other words, do not allow offensive, biased, or foul-mouthed comments), but disallowing civil criticism will quickly gain your company a reputation for silencing the collective voice of the Internet: the deadliest sin in the world of Web 2.0.

Deleting Critical Comments Leads to Trouble

Above all else, social media participants seem to hate anything that smacks of censorship. A company that refuses to post—or, worse yet, takes down or threatens to take down—comments from readers with a bone to pick will soon find themselves on the wrong end of a TwitStorm.

That's what happened to food manufacturing giant Nestle, which was targeted by Greenpeace for using palm oil in its products. First, Nestle tried to quash a Greenpeace video (the video apparently likened eating a KitKat bar to eating an orangutan). A number of Greenpeace supporters then changed their Facebook photos to look like the company's logos, only with an anti-Nestle bent, then posted critical comments on Nestle's Facebook page. Nestle threatened to take down any comments that used such logos, responding that it had the right to control content on its site. The result? More angry posts, lost customers, a public relations nightmare, and an eventual agreement by Nestle to "ensure that its products have no deforestation footprint."

This doesn't mean you have to allow complaints and critiques to stand without a response, but you should instruct employees who post for your company to take those complaints to the appropriate person or department—and to resist the urge to "take on" the dissatisfied customer in the comments field. Having a long back-and-forth on a company-sponsored site about whether a product works as advertised or how dark its "dark red" upholstery really is won't successfully promote your company.

If you decide to allow moderated comments, use alternative 1, below. As you'll see, this option also tells employees how to handle complaints and criticism that come in through the comments feature.

To disallow comments entirely, you can use alternative 2. Obviously, this option will work only for sites for which you can control the comments features, such as business blogs, some Facebook pages, and individual videos at YouTube. It may not be possible with other social media such as Twitter, for example.

Alternative 1: Moderated Comments

Handling Comments

We encourage reader responses and comments to our social media postings. However, not all reader commentary is fit to print. If you post entries that elicit reader responses or comments, you must follow these guidelines:

1. Do not allow the posting of spam, advertisements, or comments that merely link to another website (unless they are responsive to the original post).

2. Do not allow the posting of any comment that is obscene or offensive.

3. Do not allow the posting of any comment that reveals trade secrets or proprietary information. For example, if a competitor's employee reveals that company's confidential information in a comment, remove it immediately and report it to your manager.

4. Do not remove relevant anti-Company comments simply because they are negative. Do not engage in online arguments or "flame wars" through social media commenting. Talk to your manager about how—and through which medium—to respond appropriately.

5. If you receive a complaint about the company or its products in a comment, immediately notify [_department responsible for handling complaints, such as "the customer service team"_], so it can handle the situation directly.

Alternative 2: No Comments

> **Handling Comments**
>
> Because of the time and resources it would require to screen com-
> ments to our Company's blog(s), we do not post reader comments.
> Please turn off the "comments" feature of any Company blog to
> which you post content or for any other social media site at which
> you post (and for which comments can be removed).

Putting It All Together:
A Sample Company-Sponsored
Social Media Policy

Here's a sample social media policy for a training company that has
its own blogs, Facebook fan page, and Twitter account. A handful
of employees post content on the company's behalf. The company
is trying to position itself as a thought leader, and so wants to allow
comments and interaction with consumers.

Sample Company-Sponsored Social Media Policy

Our Company's Social Media Presence

Social media tools, including Company-sponsored blogs and micro-blogs, social networking sites, video or picture sharing sites, wikis, and other means of communicating online, are an important part of our Company's face to the public. These social media offer opportunities to shape opinion about our products and our company, to communicate directly with customers and clients, to provide added value for our customers, and to be part of the online conversation about important developments in our field.

We want to use social media to demonstrate the need for corporate training using statistics, studies, and current news items. We want to demonstrate that we are up-to-date on developments in our field. We also want to engage consumers by showing them the tremendous variety in training methods and media, through online video, podcasts, and other demonstrations of our work.

Who May Post

Only authorized employees may set up or post to Company-sponsored blogs or microblogs, social networking pages, or other social media. Authorization is granted by the Director of Online Marketing. Before you begin posting content, you must attend social media training.

Guidelines for Employees Who Post

1. **Be respectful.** When you post about the Company, its products and employees, customers, and competitors, use good judgment. Make sure your posts are professional and respectful. It's fine to disagree, as long as you do so in a civil way and you're not offensive.

2. **Add value.** We expect you to write about new developments and trends in your area of expertise. Don't just recycle news or posts; add your perspective and provide useful advice to enable consumers to better use our products and services.

Sample Company-Sponsored Social Media Policy (continued)

3. **Post often.** We want readers to return and see what's new at our Company, and the best way you can help make that happen is to post at least weekly.

4. **Be part of the conversation.** When appropriate, link to other sites, articles, blogs, and media on the same topic. And of course, link to our Company site when appropriate.

5. **Accuracy counts.** Before you publish a blog post or a social media entry, review it for accuracy. When writing about Company business, check with the appropriate people in-house to make sure you've got the facts straight. If you later learn you've made a mistake, say so and correct it.

6. **Avoid inappropriate topics.** We want you to generate interest, but there are many ways to do that without offending readers or placing the Company in the midst of a controversy. All company policies, including those that prohibit harassment, discrimination, and unprofessional conduct, apply with equal force to your online posts.

7. **Respect ownership of intellectual property.** Don't copy or use work by someone else (including text, photos, and video) without proper authorization and, if required, attribution. If you're referring to a copyrighted story, keep your quotes short; if you want to refer to another's work, it's best to link to it in its entirety.

8. **Keep the Company's secrets.** Don't refer to or reveal the Company's trade secrets and proprietary information. This includes stock offerings, financials, products in development, and other confidential information. If you aren't sure whether to reveal particular information in your post, speak to your manager.

9. **Maintain customer and employee privacy.** Do not mention customers by name or identifying details without authorization from your manager. If you want to discuss or mention coworkers in your posts, you must get their permission first.

Sample Company-Sponsored Social Media Policy (continued)

10. Ask—and think—before you post. Remember, your posted content represents you and the Company to the public. All of us want that representation to be positive. If you aren't certain that what you plan to post is appropriate and legal, check with your manager before you post.

Identify Yourself

When you post any type of content to Company-sponsored social media, such as our Facebook or Twitter pages, you must identify yourself by name and by your position at the Company. Anonymous posting or posting under pseudonyms or aliases is prohibited. The same rule applies if you are posting comments on behalf of the Company to one of our competitors' social media accounts, websites, or product pages.

You Are Responsible for Your Posts

Remember, you are legally responsible for what you post online, whether on a personal site or a company-sponsored site. You can be held personally liable for defaming others, revealing trade secrets, and copyright infringement, among other things. All Company policies apply to your online posts on Company-sponsored sites.

All employees who post content to Company sites and pages must include the following disclaimer:

"The posts on this page express my own views and opinion, and do not necessarily reflect the views of TrainersEdge."

Handling Comments

We encourage reader responses and comments to our social media postings. However, not all reader commentary is fit to print. If you post entries that elicit reader responses or comments, you must follow these guidelines:

Sample Company-Sponsored Social Media Policy (continued)

1. Do not allow the posting of spam, advertisements, or comments that merely link to another website (unless they are responsive to the original post).

2. Do not allow the posting of any comment that is obscene or offensive.

3. Do not allow the posting of any comment that reveals trade secrets or proprietary information. For example, if a competitor's employee reveals that company's confidential information in a comment, remove it immediately and report it to your manager.

4. Do not remove relevant anti-Company comments simply because they are negative. Do not engage in online arguments or "flame wars" through social media commenting. Talk to your manager about how—and through which medium—to respond appropriately.

5. If you receive a complaint about the Company or its products in a comment, immediately notify the customer service department, so it can handle the situation directly.

8

Cellphones

In This Chapter:

Policy Provisions for Cellphones

☐ Company-Issued Cellphones

☐ Personal Use of Company-Issued Cellphones

☐ Security of Company-Issued Cellphones

☐ Personal Cellphones at Work

☐ Don't Use a Cellphone While Driving

    ☐ Optional Policy Language for Hands-Free Equipment

☐ Using Your Cellphone for Business

ellphones have changed the landscape of everyday life so much that it's hard to remember a time when they weren't everywhere. But that time wasn't so long ago. Cellphones didn't become a common consumer purchase until the 1990s or so, and even then few people used them as a primary means of communication. Today, however, the cellphone is a necessity of modern life. By 2011, there were more cellphones than people in the United States.

The First Call on a Portable Cellphone

There was a lot going on in April 1973: France and the Netherlands recognized North Vietnam as a separate country; John Lennon and Yoko Ono formed their own country called Nutopia (its national anthem was silence, possibly preferable to the chart-topping single of the month, "Tie a Yellow Ribbon Round the Old Oak Tree," by Tony Orlando and Dawn); Richard Nixon announced the resignation of many of his top aides in the Watergate scandal; and Roberto Clemente's number was retired by the Pittsburgh Pirates. Oh, and Martin Cooper made the first public telephone call on a portable cellphone.

Of course, "portable" is in the eye of the beholder: The phone Cooper used weighed two and a half pounds and was ten inches long, and its battery died after 20 minutes. It was called "The Boot" because of its shape. At the time, Cooper worked for Motorola. He used his first phone call to contact a friend who worked at a rival company, AT&T's Bell Labs.

Unfortunately, the convenience of the cellphone can also be its curse, especially in the workplace. Cellphones can be distracting and disruptive at work, whether used in a shared workspace, during a business meeting, or while the owner should be helping customers or clients. They can even be dangerous, if used to transfer trade secrets, to eavesdrop in the company lunch room, or while driving, for example. This chapter provides some policy language you can use to prevent common cellphone problems.

 RELATED TOPIC
This chapter covers only the "phone" feature of cellphones.
Other chapters cover technologies that might be included with a cellphone, such as cameras (Chapter 10), instant messaging (Chapter 5), email (Chapter 3), and Internet connectivity (Chapter 9).

Company-Issued Phones

If your company is one of the many that issue cellphones to employees, you'll need policy language covering a few issues: company ownership of the phones, personal calls, and theft prevention.

Company Ownership of Phones

Your policy should start by telling employees that company-issued cellphones are company property, which employees must return upon request. This gives your company the ability to control the features on its cellphones (for example, to make sure that the employee's contact list can be erased remotely if the cellphone is stolen). It also establishes the company's right to inspect cellphones, if necessary, which in turn diminishes employees' expectations of privacy in company-issued cellphones.

> **Company-Issued Cellphones**
>
> The Company may issue cellphones to employees whose jobs require them to make calls while away from work or require them to be accessible for work-related matters.
>
> Cellphones issued by the Company are Company property. Employees must comply with Company requests to make their Company-issued cellphones available for any reason, including upgrades, replacement, or inspection. Employees who leave the Company for any reason must turn in their Company-issued cellphones.

Personal Use of Company Cellphones

For a variety of reasons, the simplest policy is not to allow personal calls on company cellphones. Employees and managers won't have to review cellphone bills every month looking for numbers that aren't related to business. The company won't have to make judgment calls about how much personal use of a cellphone is too much. And calls made by customers, clients, and coworkers won't go straight to voicemail because an employee is too busy chatting with friends and family to pick up a work-related call.

Despite all the good reasons not to allow personal calls, however, an outright ban is impractical. Even the most conscientious employee may occasionally have to take a brief personal call. And allowing these calls—often, from a child, spouse, or partner who needs to check in—may help employees be more productive by alleviating pressing personal concerns. The policy below reflects those considerations.

> **Personal Use of Company-Issued Cellphones**
>
> Company-issued cellphones are to be used only for business purposes. Although occasional, brief personal phone calls using a Company-issued phone are permitted, personal use that exceeds this standard will result in discipline, up to and including termination. Employees are expected to reimburse the Company for any costs or charges relating to personal use of their cellphones.

Security of Company-Issued Phones

Employees may have phones full of text messages and client contact information, and they need to know how to keep that data private. Your policy should also explain what employees should do if their company-issued phones are stolen.

> **Security of Company-Issued Phones**
>
> Employees are responsible for the security of Company-issued cellphones and the information stored on them. Always keep your cellphone with you when traveling; never leave it unattended in your car or hotel room. If your Company-issued cellphone is lost or stolen, notify the IT department immediately. Never store confidential Company information on a cellphone.
>
> When using a cellphone, remember that your conversations are not necessarily private. Those around you can hear your end of the conversation. To protect the confidentiality of Company information, please make cellphone calls in a private place.

Security of Company-Issued Phones, continued

Cellphone transmissions may be intercepted. For this reason, employees should not conduct highly sensitive or confidential conversations by cellphone. If you have any questions about what types of conversations are appropriate for a cellphone and which are not, please ask your manager.

Personal Cellphones at Work

Most of your employees probably have personal cellphones that they bring to work. Apparently the main thing employees do at work with their personal cellphones—based on surveys—is annoy each other. These workplace annoyances result from loud ringtones, inappropriate personal conversations, interruptions to meetings and presentations, and rudeness to coworkers or customers while talking on the phone.

Some companies respond to these concerns by simply banning personal cellphones at work. For most employers, however, an outright ban is overkill. Allowing personal cellphones gives employees a chance to touch base with family members and friends while on breaks or at lunch, or to receive emergency messages during the day, all without using company phones. You can probably achieve the results you want—fewer interruptions and less time wasted—while allowing employees to have their cellphones at work by simply prohibiting employees from using cellphones (or allowing them to ring) at certain times, in particular locations, or for excessive amounts of time.

The policy language below contains basic cellphone etiquette for the workplace that most companies will want to adopt. Note that this policy addresses only personal use of personal phones (for policy language on employees using their personal phones and other devices for work, see Chapter 9).

Personal Cellphones at Work

Although our Company allows employees to bring their personal cellphones to work, we expect employees to keep personal conversations to a minimum. While occasional, brief personal phone calls are acceptable, frequent or lengthy personal calls can affect productivity and disturb others. For this reason, we generally expect employees to make and receive personal phone calls during breaks only.

Employees must turn off the ringers on their cellphones while away from their cellphones. If you share workspace with others, you must turn off the ringer on your phone while at work.

Employees must turn off their cellphones or leave their phones elsewhere while in meetings, presentations, or trainings. Employees must also turn off their cellphones or leave their phones elsewhere while meeting with clients or serving customers.

It is inappropriate to interrupt a face-to-face conversation with a coworker in order to take a personal phone call.

Remember, others can hear your cellphone conversations. Try to talk quietly, and save intimate discussions for another time.

Employees who violate this policy will be subject to discipline, up to and including termination.

Annoying Ringtones: One of the Top Workplace Peeves

Since employees started bringing their cellphones to work, they've been annoying their coworkers with loud ringtones. According to a recent study by Randstad USA, employees find loud noises, including cellphone ringtones, to be one of the seven biggest pet peeves. Gossip, poor time management by coworkers, messiness in communal spaces (the Company kitchen or break room, for instance), potent scents, misuse of email, and overuse of personal communication devices—such as smartphones and cellphones—during meetings round out the list.

Safety

Studies show that drivers who are distracted cause more accidents, and that cellphones and other forms of wireless technology are increasingly to blame for our lack of attention to the road. How many accidents? According to www.distraction.gov, more than 3,000 people were killed—and 431,000 were injured—in motor vehicle accidents involving distracted drivers in 2014 alone.

Most of us know that texting or using a phone while driving can be dangerous, but it still happens. In fact, the National Highway Traffic Safety Administration reports that, at any daylight moment across the United States, 660,000 drivers are using cellphones or other electronic devices while driving—and this number has been relatively constant since 2010.

One Year, 100 Cars, 241 Drivers, and 82 Crashes

To get a better idea of why people get into car accidents, the National Highway Transportation Safety Association and the Virginia Tech Transportation Institute created an experiment: They put video and sensor equipment in 100 cars and tracked driver behavior for a year. And an eventful year it was, with more than two million miles driven, 82 crashes, 761 near-crashes, and more than 8,000 "critical incidents" (situations when the driver either got too close to another car, pedestrian, cyclist, animal, or object, or had to engage in crash avoidance behavior—swerving, braking, and so on—to stay out of trouble).

The study revealed that almost 80% of crashes involved some form of driver distraction (primarily using a cellphone) or drowsiness. A few more interesting facts:

- **Dialing a cellphone is significantly more dangerous than simply talking or listening on the phone.** But the number of accidents and near-accidents attributable to each activity was about the same because drivers spend so much more time talking and listening on a phone than dialing one.

- **Don't let a bug in the car—or try to swat it once it's there.** Reaching for a moving object makes a driver nine times more likely to get in an accident. Reading, applying makeup, and dialing a cellphone each increase the risk of an accident by a factor of three, but having an insect in the car increased the risk by a factor of seven.

- **Experience counts.** Drivers with more years of experience had far fewer crashes and near-crashes than relatively inexperienced drivers.

- **Better drivers just seem nicer.** Drivers with fewer crashes and near-crashes scored higher on tests that measured extroversion, openness to experience, agreeableness, and conscientiousness.

- **Don't hire this guy.** A relatively small number of drivers caused most of the problems: 27 of the drivers in the test were responsible for almost 75% of the crashes and near-crashes; one of them had 15 incidents in one year.

To address these concerns, a growing number of states have passed laws that limit the use of cellphones while driving. These laws take several forms: Some require drivers to use a hands-free device if they want to talk on the phone, some prohibit younger or less experienced drivers from using any type of cellphone, and some allow officers to cite drivers for using a handheld cellphone if the driver is pulled over for another offense.

> **TIP**
>
> **Keep up on the laws of your state.** For detailed information on state driving safety laws, check out the website of the Governors Highway Safety Association at www.ghsa.org. Select "State Laws & Funding" to see state law charts on a number of topics, including use of cellphones. The site, which is updated frequently, also has a number of other resources, including research and reports on various driver safety issues. Note that some local governments have also enacted cellphone restrictions, so check with your town, city, or county as well.

If your company does business in a state that limits the use of cellphones while driving, of course you'll want to require employees to follow the law. However, even companies in states that haven't legislated in this area need a cellphone policy. Simply put, using a cellphone while driving is dangerous. And, if an employee causes an accident while doing business on a cellphone, your company could be held liable for the damages.

It really doesn't matter whether your company issues cellphones to employees or not: If your company's employees do business by phone, your company needs a cellphone policy. Not only will this help protect the safety of company employees and those they might encounter on the road, but it will also help your company avoid liability for accidents.

Cellphones + Driving Employees = Company Liability

There have been plenty of big settlements in lawsuits against companies whose employees injured or killed someone while talking on a cellphone. Why are the companies sued? Because they typically have much deeper pockets than the employee who actually caused the accident. Consider these examples:

- A stockbroker from Smith Barney was making a cold call to a potential client while driving when he struck and killed a motorcyclist. Although the broker was using his own cellphone and driving to a nonbusiness event, the plaintiff argued that Smith Barney should be found liable because it encouraged employees to use their cellphones for cold calling without training them on safety issues. Smith Barney eventually settled the case for $500,000.

- A lawyer was making a business call on her cellphone while driving home from work. She hit something, which she thought was a deer, and kept driving; sadly, she actually hit—and killed—a teenager. The attorney served a year in jail for hit-and-run driving and was ordered to pay the victim's family more than $2 million; her law firm settled its part of the case for an undisclosed amount.

- An employee of International Paper was using her company cellphone when she rear-ended another driver on the freeway, causing injuries that eventually required the other driver to have her arm amputated. The company paid $5.2 million to settle the case.

- An Illinois state trooper crashed head-on into another vehicle, killing two sisters. He pleaded guilty to reckless homicide and reckless driving and was sentenced to 30 months of probation; evidence was presented that he was driving 126 miles per hour, sending email on the car's computer, and using his cellphone when the crash took place. The girls' family sued him and his employer, the State of Illinois, for $46 million in damages.

Don't Use a Cellphone While Driving

We know that our employees may use their cellphones for work-related matters, whether these devices belong to the employee or are issued by the Company.

Employees are prohibited from using cellphones for work-related matters while driving. We are concerned for your safety and for the safety of other drivers and pedestrians, and using a cellphone while driving can lead to accidents.

If you must make a work-related call while driving, you must wait until you can pull over safely and stop the car before placing your call. If you receive a work-related call while driving, you must ask the caller to wait while you pull over safely and stop the car. If you are unable to pull over safely, you must tell the caller that you will have to call back when it is safe to do so.

If your company wants to allow employees to use a hands-free device to talk on the phone while driving, you can add the language below to the end of the policy. If your company issues cellphones to employees for work-related calls, it should also issue them hands-free equipment to allow them to use the phones in accordance with this part of the policy. Keep in mind, however, that some studies have shown that the use of hands-free equipment does not significantly eliminate the risk of accidents from talking on a cellphone.

Currently, no state prohibits adult, experienced drivers from using hands-free devices while driving, except for certain professions (such as school bus drivers). Before you adopt the policy language below, check on the laws of your state and local government to make sure that hands-free devices are still allowed.

Optional Policy Language for Hands-Free Equipment

Hands-Free Equipment

Employees may use hands-free equipment to make or answer calls while driving without violating this policy. However, safety must always be your first priority. We expect you to keep these calls brief. If, because of weather, traffic conditions, or any other reason, you are unable to concentrate fully on the road, you must either end the conversation or pull over and safely park your vehicle before resuming your call.

Wage and Hour Concerns

As portable technology improves, it's becoming easier for employees to work anywhere, at almost any time. The benefits of this trend are obvious: higher productivity, opportunities for telecommuting, improved work-life balance for employees, even reducing greenhouse gases as fewer employees have to commute each day.

There's a significant legal downside to consider, however. When nonexempt employees—those who are entitled to earn overtime— work away from their usual worksite, those hours might not get recorded, and the employee may not receive overtime pay, in violation of wage and hour laws.

The Fair Labor Standards Act (FLSA) is the federal law that governs wages and hours. Among other things, the FLSA requires employers to pay nonexempt employees overtime if they work more than 40 hours in a week; some state laws have daily overtime standards. Employees must be paid for every hour the employer "suffers or permits" them to work. This rule has been interpreted fairly strictly against employers: If employees are working overtime hours, and your company knows or should know about it, the employees are entitled to overtime pay.

Recent changes to the overtime rules make many more white-collar employees eligible to earn overtime. Previously, office employees earning less than $455 a week were automatically eligible to earn overtime (that is, they were nonexempt employees). Employees earning more than $455 a week did not have to be paid overtime for working extra hours if they fit into one of the exemption categories (for example, because they were exempt as managers or as professional employees). Now, the wage cutoff has been raised to $913 a week, or $47,476 a year. Employees earning less than this amount must be paid overtime when they work extra hours, regardless of their job duties. The federal government estimates this change will make more than four million more employees eligible to earn overtime.

Cellphones can create an overtime problem because employees can use them anywhere at any time. Employees who make a few work-related calls on the weekend or after hours might be entitled to overtime. This is true whether they use their own phones or a phone issued by the company. And, it will be tough for the company to find out about these extra hours until it's too late: Often, a company only discovers that an employee thinks he or she should have earned overtime when it is served with a lawsuit or complaint from the federal or state labor department. The best way to avoid these problems is to adopt a policy prohibiting employees from making unauthorized calls on their own time.

Using Your Cellphone for Business

Our Company's overtime rules apply to any type of work done after hours, including using a Company-issued cellphone to make business calls. All overtime work—including such work-related calls—must be approved in writing, in advance. Working overtime without permission violates Company policy and may result in disciplinary action.

> ⚠ CAUTION
>
> **If they work, you must pay.** Even if your company requires employees to get approval before working overtime, it should pay for the overtime hours they work, including hours that aren't authorized. Discipline employees who work unapproved overtime, but pay them for those hours. This is a much safer approach than having to argue later, to a labor commissioner or judge, that your company didn't "suffer or permit" the work.

> ⚠ CAUTION
>
> **Don't forget the acknowledgment form.** If your company adopts the cellphone policy covered in this chapter, make sure you require employees to sign an acknowledgment form. You'll find a sample acknowledgment form and instructions at this book's online companion page; see the appendix for more information.

Putting It All Together: Sample Cellphone Policy

Here's a sample cellphone policy adopted by a company that sells and repairs office equipment. The company has issued cellphones to its sales and service staff, who make numerous work-related calls every day and are often away from the office. Because employees spend much of their day driving to and from client businesses, the company is also very concerned about driving safety, so much so that it decides not to allow cellphone use while driving, even with hands-free devices.

Sample Cellphone Policy

Company-Issued Cellphones

The Company may issue cellphones to employees whose jobs require them to make calls while away from work or require them to be accessible for work-related matters.

Cellphones issued by the Company are Company property. Employees must comply with Company requests to make their Company-issued cellphones available for any reason, including upgrades, replacement, or inspection. Employees who leave the Company for any reason must turn in their Company-issued cellphones.

Personal Use of Company-Issued Cellphones

Company-issued cellphones are to be used only for business purposes. Although occasional, brief personal phone calls using a Company-issued phone are permitted, personal use that exceeds this standard will result in discipline, up to and including termination. Employees are expected to reimburse the Company for any costs or charges relating to personal use of their cellphones.

Security of Company-Issued Phones

Employees are responsible for the security of Company-issued cellphones and the information stored on them. Always keep your cellphone with you when traveling; never leave it unattended in your car or hotel room. If your Company-issued cellphone is lost or stolen, notify the IT department immediately. Never store confidential Company information on a cellphone.

When using a cellphone, remember that your conversations are not necessarily private. Those around you can hear your end of the conversation. To protect the confidentiality of Company information, please make cellphone calls in a private place.

Sample Cellphone Policy (continued)

Cellphone transmissions may be intercepted. For this reason, employees should not conduct highly sensitive or confidential conversations by cellphone. If you have any questions about what types of conversations are appropriate for a cellphone and which are not, please ask your manager.

Personal Cellphones at Work

Although our Company allows employees to bring their personal cellphones to work, we expect employees to keep personal conversations to a minimum. While occasional, brief personal phone calls are acceptable, frequent or lengthy personal calls can affect productivity and disturb others. For this reason, we generally expect employees to make and receive personal phone calls during breaks only.

Employees must turn off the ringers on their cellphones while away from their cellphones. If you share workspace with others, you must turn off the ringer on your phone while at work.

Employees must turn off their cellphones or leave their phones elsewhere while in meetings, presentations, or trainings. Employees must also turn off their cellphones or leave their phones elsewhere while meeting with clients or serving customers.

It is inappropriate to interrupt a face-to-face conversation with a coworker in order to take a personal phone call.

Remember, others can hear your cellphone conversations. Try to talk quietly, and save intimate discussions for another time.

Employees who violate this policy will be subject to discipline, up to and including termination.

Sample Cellphone Policy (continued)

Don't Use a Cellphone While Driving

We know that our employees may use their cellphones for work-related matters, whether these devices belong to the employee or are issued by the Company.

Employees are prohibited from using cellphones for work-related matters while driving. We are concerned for your safety and for the safety of other drivers and pedestrians, and using a cellphone while driving can lead to accidents.

If you must make a work-related call while driving, you must wait until you can pull over safely and stop the car before placing your call. If you receive a work-related call while driving, you must ask the caller to wait while you pull over safely and stop the car. If you are unable to pull over safely, you must tell the caller that you will have to call back when it is safe to do so.

Using Your Cellphone for Business

Our Company's overtime rules apply to any type of work done after hours, including using a Company-issued cellphone to make business calls. All overtime work—including such work-related calls—must be approved in writing, in advance. Working overtime without permission violates Company policy and may result in disciplinary action.

Portable Computing Devices: Smartphones, Laptops, Tablets, and Beyond

In This Chapter:

Policy Provisions for Portable Computing Devices

Rules for Company-Issued Devices

☐ Personal Use of Portable Computing Devices

☐ Use of Portable Computing Devices Is Not Private

☐ Content Rules for Portable Computing Devices

☐ Security of Portable Computing Devices

☐ No Texting While Driving

☐ Overtime and Portable Computing Devices

Rules for BYOD

☐ Option 1: Don't Use Personal Mobile Devices for Work

☐ Option 2: Using Personal Mobile Devices for Work

    ☐ How Employees Will Use BYOD

    ☐ Your Personal Information

    ☐ Security of Personal Mobile Devices

    ☐ Reimbursement for Use of Your Personal Device

    ☐ No Texting While Driving

    ☐ Overtime and Personal Mobile Devices

A s processing power grows and microchip size shrinks, the tech world is witnessing a convergence of portable computing devices. Handheld personal digital assistants (PDAs) like the BlackBerry are packed with more software and memory, while laptop computers are shrinking in size. And tablets, whether for use primarily as e-book readers or mobile computers, are increasingly popular.

There is no single name for all of these portable computing devices, but whether you call them smartphones, laptops, handhelds, mobile devices, or PDAs, they have something in common: Employees use them to do their jobs remotely, at home, and on the road.

Like the other technologies discussed in this book, however, portable computing devices bring increased risk with their increased efficiency. The most significant of these risks is from the theft or loss of company information. The very portability of these devices makes them a target for thieves, and all too easy to leave behind in a cab, restaurant, hotel room, or bar (iPhone prototype, anyone?). These devices may also expose the company's network to risks (if they can link into the company servers) and provide a back door for opportunistic hackers and viruses.

Because these devices are intended to allow employees to work away from the office, they can also create potentially huge liability for overtime work that the company doesn't know about or pay for. Finally, like cellphones, these devices can lead to safety problems and legal exposure for the company if employees use them while driving.

All of these risks are present whether employees use phones and other devices provided by your company or use their own personal devices for work. But the risks are multiplied in the latter scenario, often referred to as BYOD (for "bring your own device"). If employees use their own smartphones or other mobile devices for business and pleasure, your company will have to figure out what devices and uses it will allow, how it can maintain security and ownership of its information, and how to handle employee expenses, among other things.

Although many of the same considerations apply to company-issued and personal devices, your company has a lot more control over devices it provides. The privacy and security concerns are less complicated.

Company-Provided or Personal Devices?

Not long ago, perhaps the hottest trend in workplace technology was BYOD: allowing employees to use their own mobile devices for both business and pleasure. Previously, BYOD was almost nonexistent. Companies were advised to ban employees from using their own devices (which were then primarily phones and PDAs) for work. Companies issued work phones or corporate BlackBerrys to employees who needed them, and called it a day.

But employees love their personal devices, especially their iPhones. Companies reported increased demands by employees to use the devices they like and feel comfortable with for work purposes, rather than having to double up on their devices and abandon their favorite apps and platforms.

Makes sense, right? But the security, privacy, and management concerns associated with BYOD are complex. Industry experts still disagree about how best to handle everything from protecting corporate data to reimbursing employee expenses. A lot of the legal issues and practical effects associated with BYOD are still emerging, as are the mobile management solutions that allow companies to protect their data. As a result, many companies have turned instead to CYOD (choose your own device) and COPE (company-owned, personally enabled) policies, in which the company provides the device and the employee has the ability to use it for both business and pleasure. These solutions solve the problems of device choice and duplication, while giving the company more control over its data and intellectual property.

Ultimately, your company will have to decide which strategy makes the most sense, given its culture, budget, comfort with risk, IT sophistication, and interest in staying on the technological cutting edge, among other things. The advantages and disadvantages are spelled out below. Whatever solution you choose, one thing seems clear: The days of COBO (company-owned, business-only) devices seem to be numbered, if they haven't already drawn to a close. If you issue a mobile device to employees, you should expect them to use it for personal pursuits.

Benefits and Drawbacks: BYOD

Probably the most significant benefit of adopting a BYOD policy is employee satisfaction. Surveys show that employees want to use a device they feel comfortable with for both work and play, and they don't want multiple devices. Surveys also show that employees already use their own devices for work, regardless of company policy or practice.

Employee BYOD Practices: It's Not a Pretty Picture

Whether or not your company has a BYOD policy, employees are probably using their personal mobile devices for work. That is perhaps the least troubling finding of a 2012 Harris Interactive poll commissioned by ESET. Although two-thirds of the poll's respondents said their company did not have a BYOD policy, 81% used personal devices for work anyway. (A 2015 poll by Champion Solutions Group found that the number of companies without a BYOD policy had declined to 53%.) And the ways in which employees used their devices and accessed work-related information were unsafe at any speed:

- Almost half of the respondents who use a device for work had let someone else use it.
- More than a third had not activated the auto-lock feature of the device they use for work.
- About a third said the company data and files on their device were not encrypted.

These statistics are even more troubling when you consider how often people lose their personal devices, not to mention the possibility of hacking or corruption. One-quarter of the poll's respondents said they had been subjected to hacking or a malware attack on their personal device.

BYOD also has the potential to save money, although there are a couple of caveats here. First, although the company saves money on the front end when employees supply their own devices, it may have to spend considerable money either figuring out ways to secure those devices or cleaning up after a breach. Second, if employees use their own device for work, the company may have a duty to reimburse them for job-related usage. (See "Reimbursing Employees," later in this chapter, for more information on this developing issue.)

BYOD also offers a creativity edge, particularly for forward-thinking technology companies. These days, developments in the technology field for consumers are on a faster track than enterprise or business technology developments. You can use a BYOD policy to allow your employees to use the very latest devices and apps, likely long before there is a secure corporate version available.

Security risks top the list of disadvantages to a BYOD strategy. A company can't fully mitigate these risks without employee coopera-tion; for some devices and some uses, security enhancements are still trying to catch up. Some businesses find that the risk to intellectual property and corporate data are simply too great to allow BYOD, particularly in industries in which privacy of business records is paramount (such as health and finance).

Privacy concerns for employees are another potential drawback to using BYOD. When personal files and data share space with corporate files and data, personal information is at risk of being erased in a remote wipe, viewed in a corporate investigation or audit, or otherwise exposed to the employer.

Benefits and Drawbacks: CYOD and COPE

Allowing employees to choose from a list of company-supported devices (CYOD) and expressly permitting personal use of the device (COPE) have emerged as solutions to some of the problems posed by BYOD. Employees still get to use the device they want (or at least, they get some choice in devices). They don't have to carry multiple devices, and they can work remotely when they choose. And, the company picks up some or all of the cost of the device, a considerable perk.

With CYOD and COPE, however, the company can limit the devices it will support to those that meet its needs. The company can install all of the data management and security features it wants, and it can better control how employees use the device.

The cost of these benefits is choice and innovation. Employees may not be able to use the most cutting-edge technology tools or devices until a securable version becomes available. Companies will want to limit the list of devices they support, both for security reasons and to realize economies of scale. Purchasing large numbers of a few types of devices, and becoming fully proficient in the support and protection of those devices, is likely to be less expensive and time-consuming than allowing employees to choose from a long menu of options.

Rules for Company-Issued Devices

If your company issues portable devices to employees, it should adopt policy language covering those devices. This is true whether or not your company also allows BYOD.

User Rules for Company-Issued Devices

Like other types of company-issued technology, portable computing devices can easily be put to personal use. Employees may use their company smartphones to call and text friends and family, their company laptops to send personal email and chat on the Internet, or their electronic readers to review their Great American Novel. Your company should make clear that its policies on appropriate use apply to the portable computing devices it issues. You should also cover personal use of company equipment. And, your policy must address employee privacy, too.

Personal Use

There's no way around it: Employees are likely to use portable computing devices for personal reasons. That's why your company needs a policy on personal use of these devices. Like the policies in earlier chapters for email and the Internet, the policy language in Alternative 1, below, allows limited personal use. It also requires employees to reimburse your company for more than occasional personal use. Alternative 2, below, is for companies that use COPE, in which the company is providing a single device for employees to use for both business and pleasure.

Alternative 1: Limited Personal Use

Personal Use of Company-Issued Portable Computing Devices

The Company may provide you with a portable computing device (such as a laptop computer, tablet, smartphone, personal digital assistant, or [*if your company uses an industry-specific device, add it here*]). The Company may also permit you to access its network using a portable computing device to perform your job.

The Company's portable computing devices and network are intended for business use. You may use such computing devices for occasional personal purposes, but you may do so during nonwork hours only.

If an employee's use of a Company-issued portable computing device results in fees or costs beyond what the Company would otherwise have to pay for the service, the employee will be required to reimburse the Company.

Alternative 2: Company-Owned, Personally Enabled Devices

Personal Use of Company-Issued Portable Computing Devices

The Company may provide you with a portable computing device (such as a laptop computer, tablet, smartphone, personal digital assistant, or *[if your company uses an industry-specific device, add it here]*. The Company may also permit you to access its network using a portable computing device to perform your job.

Company devices are enabled for personal use. We expect you to limit your personal use of Company-issued computing devices during work hours.

The IT department will explain how to keep your business-related data and apps separate from your personal data and apps on the device.

If an employee's use of a Company-issued portable computing device results in fees or costs beyond what the Company would otherwise have to pay for the service, the employee will be required to reimburse the Company.

Privacy

Your policy should also warn employees about the company's right to access information on a device it provides. (See Chapters 1 and 3 for information about employee privacy and company-issued equipment.)

The language you use here will depend on whether you adopt a CYOD/COPE solution or not. If you are providing devices for business reasons, and employees have a limited right to use the devices for personal pursuits, you may simply tell employees they have no privacy in what they do with, and store on, their devices.

However, if your intent is to provide one device that meets all of an employee's business and personal needs, you will need to decide how much privacy to allow for an employee's personal usage. In part, this will depend on the technology you use to manage devices. For example, if you can fully segregate personal and business data, apps, and files on the device, you might be better able to allow employees some privacy in their wholly personal activities. Remember, though, that you still might need to inspect the device, audit the device, or even hand it over as evidence in a lawsuit. Therefore, you'll need to let employees know that the privacy of their usage can't be guaranteed. The second alternative, below, assumes that usage can be fully separated into personal and business.

Alternative 1: No Privacy in Company-Provided Devices

Use of Portable Computing Devices Is Not Private

The Company has the ability to access and review all information stored on the Company's portable computing devices and network. The Company reserves the right to perform such an inspection at any time, for any reason. You should not expect that any files, records, or other data stored on the Company's equipment and network will be private, even if you attempt to protect its privacy (for example, by using a password or designating it as "personal").

Alternative 2: Privacy in COPE Devices

Use of Portable Computing Devices Is Not Private

The IT department will instruct you on how to segregate your personal data, apps, and files from the business information and apps on your device. You are responsible for following these instructions to protect the Company's data and intellectual property.

The Company has the ability to access and review all information stored on the Company's portable computing devices and network. As long as you follow the rules for keeping personal and business use of your device separate, the Company will endeavor not to monitor or access your personal information on the device.

However, the Company reserves the right to inspect the device at any time, for any reason. The Company may also be required to audit the device or review its contents as part of an investigation or other legal proceeding. Therefore, you should not expect that any files, records, or other data stored on the Company's equipment and network will be private.

Appropriate Content

You need not repeat all of the content rules for the various capabilities of portable computing devices (email, instant messaging, and Internet access, for example). Instead, you can refer back to those policies here, with a reminder that they apply to company-issued portable computing devices as well.

Content Rules for Portable Computing Devices

All of our policies and rules of conduct apply to employee use of Company-issued portable computing devices. All communications (email, texting, instant messaging, and Internet access) on Company-issued portable computing devices are subject to the Company's policies on appropriate use. This means, for example, that employees may not send harassing messages, access pornographic or gambling websites, or violate any of the Company's other rules on appropriate communications content.

Security of Company-Issued Devices

Because of their small size and portability, laptops, PDAs, and smartphones are easily lost or stolen. And, because they are often intended to allow employees to access the company's network remotely, these devices present virus and hacking threats, whether they remain in the employee's possession or fall into the wrong hands.

Employees need to know how to protect their portable devices and the data on them. Your policy should cover security issues such as encryption, theft prevention, and antivirus technology.

What Really Happens When You Lose Your Smartphone?

According to industry data, people lose their phones about once a year. Of course, some people find their phones again. Some even get their phones back from the apparently well-meaning folks who find them.

But a recent study shows that those Good Samaritans who return lost phones to their owners are not so good after all. In 2012, Symantec deliberately "lost" 50 Android phones in Los Angeles, San Francisco, Washington, New York City, and Ottawa. The phones were loaded with fake data and stored passwords, and left unlocked. Then, Symantec tracked what happened to them.

The good news: About half of the phone-finders made at least some effort to return the phone. But only after digging through it like gold miners. Here's what else the study showed:

- 95% of the finders tried to access personal or sensitive information.
- 72% looked through stored photos, and 60% tried to get on Facebook and other social media sites.
- 57% accessed the fake list of passwords for the phone's services planted by Symantec.
- More than 40% tried to access banking and corporate email accounts, and more than half tried to access a fake list of "employee salaries."

CAUTION

Don't forget your reporting obligations. According to the National Conference of State Legislatures, 47 states and the District of Columbia have enacted notification statutes, which require companies to tell consumers if their personal information has been stolen or otherwise compromised. To find out what your state requires, go to the Conference's website, www.ncsl.org. Under the "Research" tab, select "Telecommunication and IT," then "Privacy and Security."

Use the policy below to tell employees how to secure the information on their company-issued portable computing devices.

Security of Company-Issued Portable Computing Devices

Although portable computing equipment (such as laptops, tablets, personal digital assistants, or smartphones) can greatly improve our communications and efficiency, they can also pose a risk to the security of the Company's proprietary information. If these devices are lost, stolen, or hacked into, an outsider could have access to Company data or the Company's network.

To prevent theft and loss of data, employees who receive Company-issued portable computing equipment must follow these guidelines:

Employees should not download confidential Company information to a portable computing device unless it is absolutely necessary. If confidential Company information is stored on a portable computing device, you must delete that information securely as soon as you are finished using it. If you are not certain whether particular data qualifies as confidential Company information, ask your supervisor for assistance.

All data and files kept on a portable computing device must be encrypted, using Company-approved encryption software.

All Company-issued portable computing devices will require power-on passwords, which must be changed every two months. You must always log or sign off before leaving a portable computing device unattended.

Security of Company-Issued Portable Computing Devices, continued

If your Company-issued portable computing device is equipped with antivirus software, you must download or install updates to this software when instructed by the Company.

You may not download, install, or use any software programs on a Company-issued portable computing device unless that program has been approved by the IT department.

Use the same malware precautions when using a portable computing device as are required for Company computers. Do not open attachments to email or instant messages if you do not know the sender or otherwise aren't sure that the attachment is legitimate. Do not open, read, or download any file from the Internet without scanning it for viruses.

Employees are responsible for the security of portable computing devices issued to them. Keep portable computing devices in your possession whenever possible. If you must leave a portable computing device unattended, you must store it out of sight in a secure location, such as a hotel safe or locked filing cabinet at home. Never leave a portable computing device in a vehicle.

Employees must immediately notify the Company's IT department if their portable computing device is lost or stolen, so the Company may remotely delete data stored on the device.

International Employers: Don't Let Trade Secrets Slip Out at the Border

The 9th Circuit Court of Appeals recently ruled that U.S. Customs and Border Patrol agents can search the contents of a traveler's laptop even if they don't have any particular reason to suspect wrongdoing. In *U.S. v. Arnold*, No. 06-50581 (April 21, 2008), the Court found no reason to exclude evidence of child pornography that Border Patrol agents found on Michael Arnold's laptop when he arrived at Los Angeles International Airport after a trip to the Philippines. Although the Fourth Amendment of the U.S. Constitution requires reasonable suspicion to search, border searches are presumed reasonable because of the government's strong interest in preventing unwanted people and items entering the country.

Let's hope that your company's employees never find themselves in exactly this situation. Even so, if your employees take laptops, PDAs, or handheld digital devices on a foreign business trip, they risk losing those devices—and the information on them—to Border Patrol agents, who sometimes confiscate such items. Your company's proprietary information and personal data about employees or customers, may be seized.

How often are devices searched at the border? According to documents the American Civil Liberties Union received after making a Freedom of Information Act (FOIA) request, more than 6,500 devices were searched between October 2008 and June 2010. Cellphones were most likely to be searched, followed by laptops and digital cameras. And, in 280 cases, the border agents transferred data from the devices to other federal government agencies.

These numbers are relatively small, given the large number of personal devices that travel internationally every day. Nonetheless, experts advise companies to limit—and protect—the proprietary and personal data employees keep on the laptops and smartphones when crossing international borders.

Lessons From the Real World

Fall into the (liability) Gap: Stolen laptops compromise job applicant data.

Joel Ruiz applied for a job at one of Gap's clothing stores in 2006. As part of the application process, Ruiz provided personal information, including his Social Security number. In 2007, Gap notified Ruiz and 800,000 other applicants that two of its laptops, which contained their application data in unencrypted form, had been stolen. Gap offered each applicant a year of free credit monitoring and fraud assistance, along with some identity theft insurance.

Ruiz filed a class action lawsuit against Gap, claiming that the company acted negligently, violated his privacy, and committed an unfair business practice, among other things. Gap argued that Ruiz's claims should be thrown out. There was no proof that Ruiz's information had been accessed or used in any way, so he couldn't show that he had suffered actual harm—an essential element of a lawsuit.

Although the district court found that Ruiz had alleged enough harm, including an increased risk of identity theft, to continue with his suit, Ruiz eventually lost the case.

Ruiz v. Gap, Inc., 540 F.Supp.2d 1121 (N.D. Cal. 2008).

Driving Safety

Like cellphones, the use of smartphones while driving can be very dangerous. In fact, texting while driving is more dangerous than talking on the phone, according to a study by the University of Utah: Those talking on a cellphone are four times more likely to get into an accident than people driving without distractions, while texting increases the likelihood of an accident by six times. The same study also shows that texting slows driver reaction times.

No DWT

One of the hottest issues in statehouses across the country these days is DWT: driving while texting. The vast majority of states have banned it outright for all drivers, and a few more ban texting for younger drivers only.

In some states, high-profile accidents may have helped push the legislation along. In Washington, for example, a driver was using his BlackBerry and failed to see that the traffic ahead of him on Interstate 5 had stopped; he crashed into a minivan, setting off a pileup that also involved four other cars and a bus. Several months later, the Washington legislature outlawed texting by drivers.

In New Jersey, the state legislature began considering its anti-texting law within a month after Governor Jon Corzine was badly injured in a car crash. Corzine, who was in the passenger seat, wasn't wearing his seat belt. What's more, his driver—who was doing 91 mph in a 65 zone—was investigated by state troopers who wanted to know whether he was texting (with his alleged girlfriend's husband) at the time of the accident.

You can find out what your state is up to at the website of the National Conference on State Legislatures, www.ncsl.org; select "Traffic Safety" in the "Transportation" issue area under "Research." Is legislation really necessary to prevent something so obviously dangerous? Unfortunately, yes: 85% of respondents to one survey said they would not DWT if it were illegal.

Despite the somewhat obvious fact that texting while driving is dangerous, however, more than half of all drivers admit to doing it. In response, most states have enacted bans on texting while driving. And companies are adopting policies prohibiting employees from doing so, too. Just like using a cellphone, texting while driving can lead to accidents, and to liability for your company.

No Texting While Driving

Employees are prohibited from using any portable computing device, whether personal or Company-owned, for work-related matters while driving. We are concerned for your safety and for the safety of other drivers and pedestrians, and texting, checking messages, going online, or otherwise using a portable computing device while driving can lead to accidents.

If you must send or read a message while driving, you must wait until you can pull over safely and stop the car before doing so.

Lessons From the Real World

If you don't know where you're going, pull over.

An employee of Berry Electric Contracting Company got lost while driving a company van in Arlington Heights, a Chicago suburb. He was trying to use the navigation device on his BlackBerry when he ran a red light and hit another car.

The driver of the other car, a 71-year-old woman, had to undergo five surgeries as a result of the crash. She sued the company for her injuries. Right before trial, the case settled for $4.1 million, which was paid by Berry Electric's insurance carrier.

Abdon M. Pallasch, "$4 Mil. Award in BlackBerry Car Accident," *The Chicago Sun-Times*, December 9, 2006.

Wage and Hour Concerns

Personal computing devices make it possible for employees to work offsite, 24 x 7 x 365. This ability to work overtime can open your company up to significant legal exposure for wage and hour claims.

When nonexempt employees—those who are entitled to earn overtime—work away from their usual worksite, those hours might not get recorded, and the employee may not receive overtime pay, in violation of wage and hour laws. Employees who check their email after hours or work on documents from home might be entitled to overtime. And, the company might not know about these extra hours until it hears from a lawyer. (For more detailed information on overtime liability, see Chapter 7.)

Time Off? Not Really

In 2014, Harris Interactive conducted a poll for Glassdoor on employee work habits while on vacation (among other things). The results really put the lie to the notion of "time off": More than 60% of employees did some work while on vacation. One in five employees were contacted by their boss while on vacation, and one in four were contacted by a colleague about work. Perhaps as a result, 9% of employees reported that a family member complained about them working while on vacation, and 6% reported working while drinking alcohol. In another possibly related finding, 11% of employees used their time off to interview for another job (perhaps one that doesn't require them to work through their vacation).

The best way to control your company's liability is to adopt a policy requiring employees to get written authorization before using handheld computers or other portable technology outside of their usual hours.

Overtime and Portable Computing Devices

Our Company's overtime rules apply to any type of work done after hours, including using a Company-issued portable computing device (laptop, smartphone, etc.) for work. If you are eligible to earn overtime, all overtime work—including work done on a personal computing device —must be approved in writing, in advance. Working overtime without permission violates Company policy and may result in disciplinary action.

Rules for Personal Devices and BYOD

Whether or not your company will allow employees to use their own devices for work, you need to include something about BYOD in your policies. Why? Because surveys show that the majority of employees use their devices for work, even if company policy doesn't explicitly provide for it. Below, we provide a sample policy for companies that plan not to allow BYOD. Then, we provide policy language for companies that want to use BYOD in their workplaces.

Prohibiting BYOD

Given the problems BYOD poses (particularly the security risks, as discussed above), a number of companies have chosen not to allow BYOD for now. In fact, trend spotters have noted that, although BYOD seemed like a must-have strategy a couple of years ago, relatively few companies have adopted it. Some have even given up on it after initially embracing it. Prohibiting BYOD makes sense for companies in industries that don't require remote communication and networking, especially if they provide company-issued devices to any employees whose job requires them.

Whether you have considered the issues and decided against BYOD or you simply aren't ready to tackle the issue yet, you should adopt policy language prohibiting BYOD. Personal mobile devices are so common, and so popular, that employees are likely to use them for work out of convenience. The best strategy, if you don't want BYOD at your workplace, is to tell employees that it's prohibited.

Alternative 1: BYOD Prohibited

Don't Use Personal Mobile Devices for Work

We understand that employees may occasionally wish to use their own mobile devices—such as smartphones or tablets—for work. However, storing Company information on a personal mobile device or using such a device to access the Company's network creates unacceptable security risks. Therefore, employees are prohibited from using their own mobile devices for business purposes or from storing Company information on a personal mobile device. If you feel that you need a mobile device to do your job, please talk to your manager to find out whether you are eligible for a Company-issued device.

Does BYOD Save Money?

One of the primary reasons employers switch to a BYOD model is to save money. But does the math work out? Switching to BYOD can lead to increased costs in the areas of service and reimbursements. For company equipment, the company can negotiate a corporate discount; if the employer simply pays the employee's plan costs, the monthly nut is likely to be higher. Similarly, reimbursing employees leads to increased costs in time, as the employees have to submit reimbursement forms and the company has to process and pay them.

On the other hand, companies save money by not purchasing the devices in the first place. And, BYOD advocates claim that allowing employees to use their own devices for work results in greater efficiency and productivity, a benefit that's hard to put into dollars and cents. If your company is considering a BYOD policy, you should run the numbers to see which costs will increase—and which will decrease—if you make the change.

Which Devices Are Right for Your Company?

If you decide to adapt some form of BYOD policy, you'll need to tell employees which devices and platforms your company will allow. A consultation with the IT department—and perhaps an employee survey to find out which devices employees want to use—can help you answer this question. The sample policy language below addresses the most common BYOD devices. It also prohibits employees from using devices that have been altered to give users root access to the operating system, which leaves the device vulnerable to hacking and other security problems.

Alternative 2: BYOD Allowed

Using Personal Mobile Devices for Work

The Company allows employees to use their personal smartphones, tablets, and other mobile devices for work, in the circumstances set forth below. To protect the Company's data and resources, only certain devices and uses are allowed.

Acceptable Devices

Employees may do business only on the following personal devices; a device that does not appear on this list may not be used for work nor may it connect to the Company's network:

- Apple iPhones and iPads

- Android smartphones and tablets

- BlackBerry smartphones and playbooks

Employees must maintain the original operating systems on their devices; for example, they may not use personal devices that have been "rooted" or "jailbroken."

How Employees Will Use BYOD

There are a number of options for employee use of BYOD, with varying levels of security risk for your company. The best choice for your company will depend on a number of factors, including the type of work employees do remotely, your company's security needs and comfort with risk, and whether your employees are willing to give up at least some of their privacy in exchange for the convenience of using their own device for work.

Your options here will also depend on the type of software solution you choose to help you manage BYOD. For example, if your employees really want and need access to confidential corporate documents from their mobile devices and can handle the loss of privacy, a mobile device management system that gives your company total control over the employee's device, just like it would have over a traditional corporate BlackBerry, would make sense. If your employees feel strongly about the privacy of their personal information, you might limit them to accessing only business email and calendaring functions from their mobile devices, using a mobile application management system to control those applications and the data associated with them.

Ultimately, you'll have to come up with your own policy language here, after deciding how you will allow employees to use BYOD and how your company will manage the security challenges. Here are a couple of examples:

Optional Language: Email Only

Employees may use their personal devices solely to access their corporate email accounts. No Company data may be stored or downloaded to your personal computing device.

Optional Language: Corporate Documents

Employees may use their personal devices to access their corporate email accounts and certain Company databases, depending on your position and job requirements. Any Company documents on an employee's personal mobile device must be encrypted and password-protected. Such documents must be securely deleted as soon as you are finished using them.

Privacy Concerns

If you issue company equipment to an employee, such as a computer or cellphone, your company owns that property. It may inspect or take back the property when it wishes, monitor the employee's use of the property, and so on. When an employee uses a personal device for work, however, the lines are less clear. On the one hand, employees are likely to feel that their vacation photos, personal contact lists, and personal online activities are private. On the other, your company still has some interest in what the employee does with the device and the company data it holds.

How you handle this issue depends, in part, on the type of mobile device or application management software your company will use. For example, some programs have become fairly sophisticated at separating business data from personal data, so that the company can control—and if necessary, remotely wipe—its information without endangering employees' photos, downloads, and other personal items. In these programs, business data is typically segregated into one area, which can then be managed and erased.

No matter what type of system you use, you run a risk of accessing and even destroying private information. Employees must know that this risk is one of the costs of using their own device for work.

Your Personal Information

When you use a personal computing device for work, the Company may have the ability to access and review information stored on the device. The Company may also need to remotely wipe the device in case it is lost, stolen, or otherwise subject to a security breach. In this case, some or all of your personal information may be lost. You should not expect that any files, records, or other data stored on a personal device you use for work will be private.

Don't Use Daddy's Phone

The CEO of Mimecast—who played a role in developing his company's BYOD policy—fell victim to it while on vacation. He had used his BYOD smartphone to take photos of the family's trip to South Africa. However, all of those photos were remotely wiped, per company policy, when his five-year-old daughter entered the wrong password five times in a row. The company had considered a "partial wipe" policy, but ultimately decided it did not provide enough security for company information. The company surveyed 500 IT professionals and found that 21% believed BYOD had been a risk to their businesses; for 26% more, that risk was great enough to deny employees the right to use BYOD altogether.

Security of Personal Devices

Security concerns are greatly heightened when employees use their own personal devices for work. If your company issues smartphones or other devices, it can control what's on the device, what it can do, and all security features. With a personal device, you must rely on the employees themselves to implement certain security safeguards. The sample policy language below adopts a number of common security rules; you will need to adapt your policy to reflect the requirements and operation of the software solution you choose.

Reimbursing Employees

Your policy should also address whether and how your company will reimburse employees who use their personal mobile devices for work. There are a number of options here, from a flat monthly stipend to an expense reimbursement model. No matter which option you choose, however, you should make sure that employees are being fully compensated for their work-related expenses. Some states require employers to pay for all tools, equipment, and other items employees need to perform their jobs. In these states, your company could face legal challenges if its BYOD program doesn't fully cover employee costs.

If you have decided not to reimburse employees for BYOD (after making sure this is legal in your state), you don't have to say anything in your policy. If you decide to reimburse employees, you'll need to survey employees on what they pay for their phone and data plans, how much (and in what ways) they will use their devices for work, and so on. Employers who reimburse employees often do so either with a set stipend payment or a percentage expense payment. Below are examples of how you might describe each plan.

Security of Personal Mobile Devices

Although using personal mobile devices is convenient and efficient for employees, it can also pose a risk to the security of the Company's proprietary information. If these devices are lost, stolen, or hacked, an outsider could get access to the Company's network or data.

To prevent theft and loss of data, employees who use their personal mobile devices for work must follow these guidelines:

Before using a personal mobile device to connect to the Company's network or otherwise do business, employees must submit their personal device to the IT department, which will register the device and configure it with the necessary applications and tools. Employees must maintain any Company applications loaded onto their personal devices.

All personal computing devices used for work must be password-protected. [*Provide additional guidance on your Company's password policy here, such as "Passwords will expire every two months, and you may not choose a password you have used in the past. The device must automatically lock after ten failed login attempts."*]

Use the same malware precautions when using a personal device for business as are required for Company computers. You must keep your antivirus software up to date and use it.

Employees are responsible for the security of the personal devices they use for business. Keep the device with you whenever possible. Always log or sign off before leaving a personal device unattended. Do not allow others to use a personal device you use for work.

Employees must immediately notify the Company's IT department if their personal computing device is lost or stolen, so the Company may remotely lock or wipe the device.

Lessons From the Real World

California employers who use BYOD must reimburse employees.

Colin Cochran was employed by Schwan's Home Service as a customer service manager. He brought a class action lawsuit on behalf of 1,500 customer service managers who were required to use their personal cellphones for work.

The trial court refused to certify his case as a class action. To be certified, a case must be appropriate for representative proceedings: It's only fair for the court to adjudicate the rights of people who aren't present if the person bringing the lawsuit can represent their interests adequately and the claims are similar enough to be decided as a group. The court ruled against Cochran because it wasn't clear that all of the class members had out-of-pocket expenses due to the policy. For example, if some members had unlimited data plans, using their phones for work wouldn't cost them anything extra. Therefore, the court found that this issue would have to be decided individually for each class member.

The court of appeals disagreed. California law requires employers to indemnify employees for all necessary expenses incurred in doing their jobs. This prevents employers from passing the costs of business on to employees, rather than paying those costs themselves. Therefore, the court found, reimbursement is always required, regardless of the employee's losses. "Otherwise, the employer would receive a windfall because it would be passing its operating expenses onto the employee." Under this decision, employers in California must pay "some reasonable percentage" of employee device bills, if they require BYOD.

Cochran v. Schwan's Home Service, No. B247160 (Cal. Court of Appeals 2014).

Optional Language: Stipend Payment

Reimbursement for Use of Your Personal Device

Employees who use their personal mobile devices for work will be paid a set amount each month for work-related communications. The amount depends on how you use your device:

Phone only: Employees who use their devices only for telephone calls (or whose phones don't have a data plan and/or can't receive emails) will receive _____ per month.

Smartphone: Employees who use their devices for phone calls, texts, emails, and other work-related communications will receive _____ per month.

The Company anticipates that the above amounts will be sufficient to cover all work-related communication needs. If you believe you are not being fully reimbursed for all business use of your device, please speak to your manager.

Optional Language: Percentage Reimbursement

Reimbursement for Use of Your Personal Device

Employees who use their personal mobile devices for work will be reimbursed a percentage of their monthly costs each month. Employees are responsible for paying the full cost of [*list services and fees you won't pay, such as "roaming charges, personal applications, and fees for exceeding the usage limit on your plan."*]

Employees must submit their bills each month for reimbursement. Employees may be reimbursed _____% of their costs, up to a limit of _____ per month.

Driving Safety

As is true of company-issued devices, employees should not use their own devices while driving. (Chapter 8 covers the use of cellphones, whether owned by the employee or the company, while driving.) Use the policy language in this chapter for company-issued devices to prohibit use of BYOD devices while driving.

Wage and Hour Concerns

Even more than for company-issued devices, personal devices make it way too easy for employees to work overtime without the company knowing about it. The policy language for company-issued devices, supplied above, should be included in a BYOD policy as well.

> CAUTION
> **Don't forget the acknowledgment form.** If your company adopts the portable computing device policy covered in this chapter, make sure you require employees to sign an acknowledgment form. You'll find a sample acknowledgment form and instructions at this book's online companion page; see the appendix for more information.

Putting It All Together: Sample Portable Computing Device Policy

Here's a sample portable computing device policy adopted by a manufacturing company. Although a handful of company executives need business phones when they travel and to connect with the company's servers remotely, the vast majority of company employees do not need mobile devices to do their jobs. After much thought, the company decides to forego BYOD for now, and instead purchase corporate BlackBerrys for the executive team.

Sample Portable Computing Device Policy

Personal Use of Company-Issued Portable Computing Devices

The Company may provide you with a portable computing device (such as a laptop computer, tablet, smartphone, or personal digital assistant). The Company may also permit you to access its network using a portable computing device to perform your job.

The Company's portable computing devices and network are intended for business use. You may use such computing devices for occasional personal purposes, but you may do so during nonwork hours only.

If an employee's use of a Company-issued portable computing device results in fees or costs beyond what the Company would otherwise have to pay for the service, the employee will be required to reimburse the Company.

Use of Portable Computing Devices Is Not Private

The Company has the ability to access and review all information stored on the Company's portable computing devices and network. The Company reserves the right to perform such an inspection at any time, for any reason. You should not expect that any files, records, or other data stored on the Company's equipment and network will be private, even if you attempt to protect its privacy (for example, by using a password or designating it as "personal").

Content Rules for Portable Computing Devices

All of our policies and rules of conduct apply to employee use of Company-issued portable computing devices. All communications (email, texting, instant messaging, and Internet access) on Company-issued portable computing devices are subject to the Company's policies on appropriate use. This means, for example, that employees may not send harassing messages, access pornographic or gambling websites, or violate any of the Company's other rules on appropriate communications content.

Sample Portable Computing Device Policy (continued)

Security of Company-Issued Portable Computing Devices

Although portable computing equipment (such as laptops, tablets, personal digital assistants, or smartphones) can greatly improve our communications and efficiency, they can also pose a risk to the security of the Company's proprietary information. If these devices are lost, stolen, or hacked into, an outsider could have access to Company data or the Company's network.

To prevent theft and loss of data, employees who receive Company-issued portable computing equipment must follow these guidelines:

Employees should not download confidential Company information to a portable computing device unless it is absolutely necessary. If confidential Company information is stored on a portable computing device, you must delete that information securely as soon as you are finished using it. If you are not certain whether particular data qualifies as confidential Company information, ask your supervisor for assistance.

All data and files kept on a portable computing device must be encrypted, using Company-approved encryption software.

All Company-issued portable computing devices will require power-on passwords, which must be changed every two months. You must always log or sign off before leaving a portable computing device unattended.

If your Company-issued portable computing device is equipped with antivirus software, you must download or install updates to this software when instructed by the Company.

You may not download, install, or use any software programs on a Company-issued portable computing device unless that program has been approved by the IT department.

Sample Portable Computing Device Policy (continued)

Use the same malware precautions when using a portable computing device as are required for Company computers. Do not open attachments to email or instant messages if you do not know the sender or otherwise aren't sure that the attachment is legitimate. Do not open, read, or download any file from the Internet without scanning it for viruses.

Employees are responsible for the security of portable computing devices issued to them. Keep portable computing devices in your possession whenever possible. If you must leave a portable computing device unattended, you must store it out of sight in a secure location, such as a hotel safe or locked filing cabinet at home. Never leave a portable computing device in a vehicle.

Employees must immediately notify the Company's IT department if their portable computing device is lost or stolen, so the Company may remotely delete data stored on the device.

Don't Use Personal Mobile Devices for Work

We understand that employees may occasionally wish to use their own mobile devices—such as smartphones or tablets—for work. However, storing Company information on a personal mobile device or using such a device to access the Company's network creates unacceptable security risks. Therefore, employees are prohibited from using their own mobile devices for business purposes or from storing Company information on a personal mobile device. If you feel that you need a mobile device to do your job, please talk to your manager to find out whether you are eligible for a Company-issued device.

No Texting While Driving

Employees are prohibited from using any portable computing device, whether personal or Company-owned, for work-related matters while driving. We are concerned for your safety and for the safety of other

Sample Portable Computing Device Policy (continued)

drivers and pedestrians, and texting, checking messages, going online, or otherwise using a portable computing device while driving can lead to accidents.

If you must send or read a work-related message while driving, you must wait until you can pull over safely and stop the car before doing so.

Overtime and Portable Computing Devices

Our Company's overtime rules apply to any type of work done after hours, including using a portable computing device (laptop, smartphone, etc.) for work. If you are eligible to earn overtime, all overtime work—including work done on a personal computing device—must be approved in writing, in advance. Working overtime without permission violates Company policy and may result in disciplinary action.

Cameras and Recording Devices

Phones are not the only digital devices that incorporate cameras: You can also find cameras on PDAs (personal digital assistants), MP3 players, and even binoculars. These days, cameras and recording devices (for audio and video) are also showing up in wearable technology, from Google Glass and other headset-style gadgets to smart watches and even smart rings.

So far, camera phones are certainly the most prevalent and, as a result, have brought us many images we might never have seen otherwise, captured by people who just happened to have their phones with them. These images have exposed scandals, captured natural disasters, and caught celebrities in compromising positions. They've given rise to the "citizen journalist," ready to provide evidence of breaking events as they happen.

You Can Thank the Camera Phone

Don't believe that camera phones have already had a major impact on the way we see the world? Consider these images, all captured on camera phone:

- the execution of Saddam Hussein
- the London Tube bombing
- police shootings leading to the Black Lives Matter Movement
- the Asian tsunami
- the shootings at Virginia Tech, and
- some of the images of prisoner abuse from Abu Ghraib.

Of course, not all of the famous photos taken with camera phones are this weighty. You can also toss into the pile a picture of French soccer star Zinedine Zidane smoking a cigarette, after having starred in an antismoking campaign; pictures of Prince Harry dressed as a Nazi for a costume party; and the video of Michael Richards (who played Kramer on "Seinfeld") going off on a racist rant in a Los Angeles nightclub.

The very features that make camera phones and other mobile and wearable recording devices so cool—their small size, portability, and dual function, which allow users to record and capture images on the sly—also make them a very real workplace danger. Employers have become increasingly worried about employees violating their coworkers' privacy by recording them surreptitiously at work. Employers that have trade secrets to protect—whether in the form of documents, devices, processes, or personnel—are also understandably afraid that employees might use a camera phone or other recording device to capture and transmit confidential information.

Whether your company's resident photographer is capturing dirty dancing at the company's holiday party or trade secrets on the factory floor ("Let's take a group photo … in front of the dye mixer!"), a camera or other recording device makes it possible for images and information to leave your company in a snap. This chapter explains your policy options for dealing with cameras and other recording devices in the workplace. Alternative 1 is an outright ban; Alternative 2 allows employees to bring their cameras and recording devices to work, but provides some restrictions on how and where employees may use them.

Alternative 1: Banning Cameras and Recording Devices

The first decision you'll have to make is whether your company should prohibit photographic and recording devices—cameras, video cameras, and camera phones, and wearable tech products with recording capability—outright. Note that banning cameras is different from limiting their use, described below in "Alternative 2: Use Restrictions." A ban means employees may not bring these devices to the workplace, period.

Camera Bans: More Common Than You Might Think

Banning all cameras and recording devices in the workplace may seem like an extreme reaction to a somewhat theoretical problem. For some companies, that's exactly what it is. But the problems associated with secretly recording others are very real, especially in situations where privacy is at a premium. For example, many fitness clubs, gyms, and swimming pools have banned cameras and camera phones after naked locker room photos began circulating on the Internet. Certain nightclubs and other hot spots where celebrities like to mingle ban camera phones. Some hospitals and courthouses also ban camera phones, as do some companies (including camera phone manufacturers). And a number of establishments, including movie theaters, strip clubs, cafes, restaurants, and bars, officially banned Google Glass, even before the device was commercially available.

This is a very restrictive policy choice, suitable only for certain employers. A ban may be appropriate if:

- your company works on matters related to national security
- your company has strong confidentiality concerns (such as conversations about top-secret products that can be recorded) or valuable trade secrets that can be photographed—for example, machinery, processes, or secret construction, or
- your business provides opportunities for personal privacy violations—for example, employees shower on site after handling hazardous materials.

Because so many cellphones come with a camera feature, an outright ban on all recording devices will pose a real hardship for employees. That's why you'll need to include an exception clause, giving employees who need their personal phones at work a way to get permission to have them.

No Cameras and Other Recording Devices

The use of cameras, video and audio recording devices, or digital devices (such as cellphones, MP3 players, or PDAs) that have recording capability can cause violations of privacy and breaches of confidentiality.

For that reason, we do not allow cameras, video or audio recording equipment, or cellphones or other digital devices that have these capabilities, on Company property. If you have such a device with you, you may either leave it in your car or [_provide another option, such as "with the receptionist" or "with the office manager"_].

If you believe that your personal circumstances require you to have your cellphone at work, and your cellphone has a camera or other recording capability, please talk to your supervisor.

Gadgets Without Cameras = Big Corporate Sales Opportunities

After a couple of years when it was almost impossible to find a cellphone without a camera, manufacturers of cellphones and other handheld devices have started realizing that there's a large potential market for camera-free gadgets. In 2007, for example, Research in Motion released the BlackBerry 8800, a model intended especially for corporate and business use. Because some businesses continue to ban cameras, at least in some work areas, this trend shows no sign of stopping. In 2015, BlackBerry released its Classic model with no camera, and camera-less phones are available from most major carriers and manufacturers.

⊘ CAUTION

A ban on cameras at work may violate labor laws. The NLRB has found that an employee handbook banning all recording and photographs at work unduly restricts employee rights to document work conditions, such as safety violations. The Board stated that the employer, a fast food chain, had not shown any business justification for such a broad ban. It's unclear whether a company with valuable trade secrets or strong privacy concerns would fare any better before the NLRB. If you are considering a complete ban on workplace cameras (or on employee use of them at work), you should talk to an attorney.

Alternative 2: Use Restrictions

Many companies won't need to ban cameras and other recording devices outright. Instead, you might want to prohibit employees from bringing them into certain areas, prohibit employees from using these features at work, and/or set some guidelines for taking photos or recording video or audio at work.

Prohibiting Devices in Certain Areas

Most companies can use this policy language, at least for restrooms. Adapt the policy to your workplace by including all areas where cameras could pose a security or privacy risk.

Restrictions on Camera Phones and Other Recording Devices

Employees may not bring cameras, video and audio recording devices, or digital devices (such as cellphones, MP3 players, or PDAs) that have recording capability, to any of the following areas: restrooms, [*other private or secure areas, such as "locker rooms," "changing rooms," "lab," "R & D," "shop floor," and so on*].

Lessons From the Real World

It's a bird! It's a plane! It's a plane photographing our trade secrets!
In March 1969, employees at DuPont's plant in Beaumont, Texas,
noticed a plane circling overhead. DuPont later discovered that
the plane held Rolfe and Gary Christopher, who had been hired to
photograph new construction at the plant. The Christophers refused
to tell DuPont's investigators who had hired them or what they
planned to do with the photographs.

   DuPont sued the Christophers, claiming they had stolen the company's
trade secrets and sold them. DuPont claimed that the photographs
depicted an area where DuPont planned to begin producing methanol
using a confidential, unpatented process. Because the plant was under
construction when the photographs were taken, parts of the process were
visible from the air—and DuPont claimed that someone could use this
information to piece together its top-secret procedures.

   The Christophers argued that they couldn't be sued for trade secret
theft because they hadn't violated any laws or any duty to DuPont. They
were in public airspace when they took the pictures. Because they
didn't work for DuPont, they had no legal obligation to protect its
trade secrets. In short, the Christophers argued that they had gotten
hold of the photos fair and square, even if they did reveal DuPont's
methanol process.

   The Court ruled in favor of DuPont, finding that the Christophers
had taken its trade secret by "improper means." Had the Christophers
or their unnamed client used reverse engineering or independent
research to figure out DuPont's process, that would have been fine. But
taking it from DuPont without permission, at a time when DuPont was
taking precautions to keep the secret, was not.

   E.I. DuPont DeNemours & Co. v. Christopher, 431 F.2d 1012 (5th Cir. 1970).

Prohibiting Use of Cameras and Recording Devices

Some companies choose to allow employees to bring their camera phones and other devices to work, but prohibit use of their recording capabilities. This approach makes sense for many companies, particularly if an outright ban would be met with strong resistance. If your company has privacy and trade secret concerns, you can combine this language with the language above that bans cameras in certain areas, such as restrooms and laboratories.

This type of policy will be difficult to enforce; it can be tough to tell whether someone is actually taking a picture or recording with a camera phone. It will work only if your company has a relatively high level of trust in its employees.

Street Harassment Victims Fight Back—With Camera Phones

First came the camera phone, then the camera-phone voyeur, then the camera-phone crime fighter. You may have heard about "upskirt" photos—or their close relative, "downblouse" photos—taken with camera phones. Typically, these photos are taken surreptitiously. So why have we heard of them? Because there are entire websites devoted to them, where amateur voyeurs can post their photos.

Now, the public harassment tables have turned, with the advent of the antiharassment website. These sites, like Holla Back (www.ihollaback.org), allow readers to post camera phone photos of people who have harassed them in public, along with a narrative of exactly what happened. The blog's motto: If you can't slap 'em, snap 'em.

**Optional Policy Language to Prohibit Use
of Cameras and Recording Devices**

No Use of Camera Phones and Other Recording Devices at Work

Employees may not use any cameras, video and audio recording
devices, or video or recording features of cellphones, MP3 players,
PDAs, or other digital devices that contain such capability, at work.

Guidelines for Use

Your company may wish to allow employees to use their camera phones
and other devices, either in areas where your policy doesn't prohibit
such use or only in some situations—for example, at company events
or to capture candid photos for a company newsletter. If so, it's a good
idea to provide guidelines for taking and using pictures, especially of
other employees. This will help you protect employee privacy.

CAUTION

Don't forget the acknowledgment form. If your company
adopts the camera phone policy covered in this chapter, make sure you
require employees to sign an acknowledgment form. You'll find a sample
acknowledgment form and instructions at this book's online companion
page; see the appendix for more information.

Guidelines for Camera and Recording Device Use

Employees who use cameras, camera phones, or other digital devices to capture photos, audio, or video on Company property or at Company events must follow these rules:

1. Employees may record or take pictures of other employees, customers, clients, or visitors only with their permission. If you intend to publicize the pictures or other recordings—for example, by posting them on the Internet, using them in a Company newsletter, or submitting them to a photography contest—you must disclose this to the subjects.

2. Employees may not record or take pictures of Company trade secrets or other confidential information. This includes, but is not limited to, [*list the most common types of trade secrets your company has, such as "customer lists," "pricing information," "recipes," "design plans," "software code," and so on*].

3. Employees may not take or use pictures or recordings to harass others. All Company policies—including the Company's policies on harassment, discrimination, and threats—apply to workplace photographs and recordings.

4. If you have any questions about whether it's appropriate to record or take a photograph at work or use a workplace photograph or recording in a particular way, please ask your supervisor.

Putting It All Together:
Sample Camera and Recording Device Policy

Here's a sample camera and recording device policy adopted by a
(fictional) company that manufactures packaging material. Many
employees have cellphones with a camera feature, so the company
doesn't want to ban camera phones outright. Also, employees often
use their camera phones to take pictures of company parties and
employee gatherings for the company's newsletter. But the company
is also concerned about employee privacy: Employees change
into protective gear at work. And the company wants to keep its
manufacturing process confidential. The company decides to prohibit
employees from bringing cameras and other recording devices into
certain areas, and to adopt guidelines for their use at work.

Sample Camera Phone and Recording Devices Policy

Restrictions on Camera Phones and Other Recording Devices

Employees may not bring cameras, video and audio recording devices, or digital devices (such as cellphones, MP3 players, or PDAs) that have recording capability, to any of the following areas: restrooms, locker rooms, the research and development department, and Areas A through D of the plant facility.

Guidelines for Camera and Recording Devices Use

Employees who use cameras, camera phones, or other digital devices to capture photos, audio, or video on Company property or at Company events must follow these rules:

1. Employees may record or take pictures of other employees, customers, clients, or visitors only with their permission. If you intend to publicize the pictures or other recordings—for example, by posting them on the Internet, using them in a Company newsletter, or submitting them to a photography contest—you must disclose this to subjects.

2. Employees may not record or take pictures of Company trade secrets or other confidential information. This includes, but is not limited to, the manufacturing line and equipment, specifications for Company products, memos and notes from meetings regarding Company products, all information about products in development, customer lists, and any documents or photographs that have been marked "Confidential: For Internal Use Only."

3. Employees may not take or use pictures or recordings to harass others. All Company policies—including the Company's policies on harassment, discrimination and threats—apply to workplace photographs and recordings.

4. If you have any questions about whether it's appropriate to record or take a photograph at work or use a workplace photograph or recording a particular way, please ask your supervisor.

How to Use the Downloadable Forms on the Nolo Website

T his book comes with interactive files that you can access online at:

www.nolo.com/back-of-book/TECH.html

To use the files, your computer must have specific software programs installed. The files in this book are provided as RTFs. You can open, edit, print, and save these form files with most word processing programs such as Microsoft *Word*, Windows *WordPad*, and recent versions of *WordPerfect*.

Editing RTFs

Here are some general instructions about editing RTF forms in your word processing program. Refer to the book's instructions and sample agreements for help about what should go in each blank.

- **Underlines.** Underlines indicate where to enter information. After filling in the needed text, delete the underline. In most word processing programs you can do this by highlighting the underlined portion and typing CTRL-U.
- **Bracketed and italicized text.** Bracketed and italicized text indicates instructions. Be sure to remove all instructional text before you finalize your document.
- **Alternative text.** Alternative text gives you the choice between two or more text options. Delete those options you don't want to use. Renumber numbered items, if necessary.
- **Optional text.** Clauses marked "optional" can be included in the policies if you wish. Delete any optional text you do not want to include, and delete the italicized instructions.
- **Signature lines.** Signature lines should appear on a page with at least some text from the document itself.

Every word processing program uses different commands to open, format, save, and print documents, so refer to your software's help documents for help using your program. Nolo cannot provide technical support for questions about how to use your computer or your software.

CAUTION
In accordance with U.S. copyright laws, the forms and audio files provided by this book are for your personal use only.

List of Forms Available on the Nolo Website

To download any of the files listed below (specific tech policies), go to:

www.nolo.com/back-of-book/TECH.html

Form Title	File Name
Computer and Software Use Policy	Software.rtf
Email Policy	Email.rtf
Internet Policy	Internet.rtf
Instant Messaging Policy	IM.rtf
Blogs and Personal Posting Policy	Blogs.rtf
Cellphone Policy	Cell.rtf
Portable Computing Device Policy	PortableComputingDevice.rtf
Camera and Recording Device Policy	Camera.rtf
Electronic Communications and Equipment Policy Acknowledgment Form	Acknowledgment.rtf
Company-Sponsored Social Media Policy	SocialMedia.rtf

Index

⚖ NOLO *Online Legal Forms*

Nolo offers a large library of legal solutions and forms, created by Nolo's in-house legal staff. These reliable documents can be prepared in minutes.

Create a Document

- **Incorporation.** Incorporate your business in any state.
- **LLC Formations.** Gain asset protection and pass-through tax status in any state.
- **Wills.** Nolo has helped people make over 2 million wills. Is it time to make or revise yours?
- **Living Trust (avoid probate).** Plan now to save your family the cost, delays, and hassle of probate.
- **Trademark.** Protect the name of your business or product.
- **Provisional Patent.** Preserve your rights under patent law and claim "patent pending" status.

Download a Legal Form

Nolo.com has hundreds of top quality legal forms available for download—bills of sale, promissory notes, nondisclosure agreements, LLC operating agreements, corporate minutes, commercial lease and sublease, motor vehicle bill of sale, consignment agreements and many more.

Review Your Documents

Many lawyers in Nolo's consumer-friendly lawyer directory will review Nolo documents for a very reasonable fee. Check their detailed profiles at **Nolo.com/lawyers**.

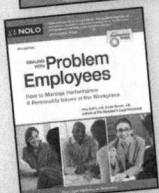

⚖ NOLO *Save 15%* off your next order

Register your Nolo purchase, and we'll send you a
coupon for 15% off your next Nolo.com order!

Nolo.com/customer-support/productregistration

On Nolo.com you'll also find:

Books & Software

Nolo publishes hundreds of great books and software programs for consumers and
business owners. Order a copy, or download an ebook version instantly, at Nolo.com.

Online Legal Documents

You can quickly and easily make a will or living trust, form an LLC or corporation, apply
for a trademark or provisional patent, or make hundreds of other forms—online.

Free Legal Information

Thousands of articles answer common questions about everyday legal issues
including wills, bankruptcy, small business formation, divorce, patents,
employment, and much more.

Plain-English Legal Dictionary

Stumped by jargon? Look it up in America's most up-to-date source for
definitions of legal terms, free at nolo.com.

Lawyer Directory

Nolo's consumer-friendly lawyer directory provides in-depth profiles of lawyers all
over America. You'll find all the information you need to choose the right lawyer.

TECH5